The Spine of the
ARCTIC

The Spine of the
ARCTIC

*A Solo Canoe Expedition through
Alaska's Brooks Range*

Geoffrey McRae Smith

gatekeeper press™

Tampa, Florida

The Spine of the Arctic:
A Solo Canoe Expedition through Alaska's Brooks Range

Published by Gatekeeper Press
7853 Gunn Hwy., Suite 209
Tampa, FL 33626
www.GatekeeperPress.com

ISBN (paperback): 9781662940170
eISBN: 9781662940187

I dedicate this book to Bernd Gaedeke and his wife, Patricia, who I was not able to properly thank for all the kindness and generosity they showed me.

Table of Contents

In the far north lies the Brooks Range, one of the most formidable and unknown mountain expanses of the continent.

Sigurd Olsen—*Runes of the North*

Preface

It was June 30, 1985. We proceeded slowly over the slick and washboard surface of the Oil Pipeline Haul Road that leads to Prudhoe Bay and the Beaufort Sea. Our small trucks were covered with a thick layer of mud. Moisture formed in rivulets on the windshield and the country was shrouded in a foggy mist. Mosquitoes swarmed us instantly and the wind-driven mist penetrated to the skin when we left the protection of our vehicles. We had traveled most of the early morning but took a rest along the road before continuing.

It was midafternoon before we reached the Arctic Circle. This is one of the few places in North America where the circle can be crossed on a formal road. I would not be south of the circle again until August 27,  1985. It was past 5:00 p.m. by the time we made first contact with the Middle Fork of the Koyukuk River. This was going to be the starting point of my journey—the journey that would cover 650 miles through Alaska's Brooks Range and end on the arctic coast at Kotzebue, Alaska, over seven weeks later. I was excited but somewhat apprehensive because of the weather and insects. I had heard of Alaskan summers when the sun never shines. June had been that kind of month: cold and rainy—no real spring, and the idea of being alone for six to eight weeks in such a remote wilderness did not sit well with me either. But I would meet people along the route and through extensive preparation, including an excellent medical kit, I felt confident that I had some of the best equipment available and a good firsthand knowledge of the country I was to enter. Beyond this, I would have to rely on my experience, fortitude, adaptability, and luck to make this trip a success.

The trip was a challenge I needed at this time in my life. I was struggling in a graduate program at the University of Alaska Fairbanks (UAF) and I was in a relationship that seemed to be evaporating. But even more than these reasons, I wanted to be in the backcountry long enough to feel a part of it, to feel and live by its rhythms, to see and sense its changes and moods. I was sure I would sense changes in myself as well.

I did not necessarily plan this expedition as a solo venture, but after approaching several people, it became obvious that to find a partner this late in the year who could commit to the trip would be difficult. Realizing this and reading Jim dale Vickery's fine article on solo paddling called "Going Alone" (*Canoe*, May/June 1985), I became excited about doing this trip alone. I bought a Mad River solo canoe called a Courier specifically for the journey. It was constructed of Kevlar©, making it a light 45 pounds for its 15-foot length.

The idea for a trip of this nature began when I worked as a Park Ranger for Kobuk Valley National Park. Part of my job was exploring the Northern tributaries of the Kobuk River. We used a 400-pound V-hulled boat with a 35-horsepower motor to move up these rivers. To my surprise, we were able to go considerable distances by pulling the boat through the shallow riffle areas. This was very strenuous work but how much easier it would be to use a shallow water craft such as a canoe.

Brooks Range rivers generally flow through wide glaciated valleys characterized by moderate elevation gradients. Rapids are rare. Also many low and relatively flat passes exist in the range, allowing easy passage from one drainage to another. These facts I knew from my personal experience and studying maps of the area.

There were areas in the Brooks Range that long intrigued me. One of these was Survey Pass—a broad plain, 3,500 feet in elevation and the headwaters region of the Alatna, Nigu, and Killik Rivers. Also I had always wanted to float the Noatak River since coming to Alaska in 1982 to work for Gates of the Arctic National Park and Preserve and I wanted to do a unique trip which few or no people had attempted. Studying a map of Alaska made up of the 3-D series of the 250,000 scale quadrangles, I noticed a natural corridor through the Brooks Range, heading to the Noatak River. The corridor included the valleys of the Alatna River, Nigu River, Flora Creek, and the Aniuk River, providing a good mixture of boreal forest and arctic habitats. I proceeded to amass maps of the route and take a closer look. I needed to work out another problem: cost. Fortunately, my UAF graduate advisor, Tim Tilsworth, asked me to be part of an Alaska Department of Transportation fishery study to look at the effects of road culverts on the arctic grayling spawning migration during the high spring runoff period. This two-week project was perfect timing for me and it paid well. Also, to save money, I wanted to avoid the high cost of hiring a bush plane to get into the Brooks Range Wilderness to begin my trip.

For a long time, I felt the Oil Pipeline Haul Road (Dalton Highway) could provide an inexpensive starting point for many extensive wilderness trips into the Range. The highway begins at the Elliott Highway, north of Fairbanks, and ends at Deadhorse near the Arctic Ocean and the Prudhoe Bay oil fields. It cuts through the Brooks Range and is flanked on the east by the 19,640,000-acre Arctic National Wildlife Refuge and on the west by the 8,472,506-acre Gates of the Arctic National Park and Preserve. I knew that I could reach the Bettles Ranger Station by floating west down the Koyukuk River from the Haul Road and if I was willing to go upstream, I could then proceed into the Range via the John River. But I wanted to travel on the Alatna River. I could either continue down the Koyukuk to the mouth of the Alatna and proceed upstream from there or I could go up the John River for a distance and cross over to the Alatna through a series of small indistinct drainages. I chose the latter. My route was set.

The Route

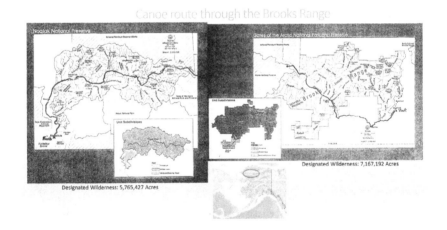

Canoe route through the Brooks Range

Designated Wilderness: 5,765,427 Acres

Designated Wilderness: 7,167,192 Acres

I planned to float down the Middle Fork of the Koyukuk River from the Haul Road to Bettles, Alaska. I would then travel up the John River to the Malamute Fork of the John and move up this to my first portage. This would take me to a series of small drainages that are part of the East Fork of Henshaw Creek. From there I would work my way into the Malamute Fork of the Atlanta River and float this to the Alatna River proper. I would travel upstream to the headwaters of the Alatna and to Survey Pass. I would portage across the Continental Divide and enter the Nigu River. A float down the Nigu would lead me to the portage to Etivlik Lake. Another portage would bring me to the Flora Creek Headwaters and into Noatak National Preserve. I would float Flora Creek to the Aniuk River and float the Aniuk to the Noatak River. I would follow the Noatak to the Noatak Delta and Kotzebue Sound. A 10-mile open ocean paddle would land me at Kotzebue and the finish of my trip.

CHAPTER 1

On the Water

It had stopped raining by the time we reached the Koyukuk River. The fog had lifted but the sky remained overcast. A cool wind blew which gave relief from the mosquitoes. A college friend, Jeff Chapman, his wife, Robin, and her brother and sister had accompanied me up the Haul Road. Now Jeff and his brother-in-law helped me move my stuff to the river's edge. We said our heartfelt goodbyes. They wished me luck and headed south back down the Haul Road. Jeff would drive my truck back to Fairbanks and park it near the apartment building where I used to live. I immediately started to arrange my equipment in the canoe with great care. The moment had arrived. I was ready. I stepped into the canoe and pushed it off the bar into silty water and slipped into the seat. The current grabbed the canoe quickly and I was on my way. The river was high and swift due to the rain. It appeared to be rising but I was encouraged because most of the gravel bars were still exposed.

It felt good to finally dig my paddle deep into

the turbulent water and feel my canoe move forward ahead of the current. Weeks of planning and preparation had focused on this time and place. I paddled hard for several hours. My arm and back muscles ached; they were not used to the new strain.

The river was initially braided into many channels but soon converged into one powerful channel. The river's force had cut steep bluffs along wide sweeping bends. Rough-legged hawks nested on the higher, more precipitous bluffs. Their warning calls could be heard for many bends as I approached the area underneath their nests. They circled in the sky. Sometimes they made shallow dives to ward me off. A black bear crossed the river 100 yards in front of me. It showed no indication that it knew I was there except in the deliberateness of its actions. I made good time on the swift current and stopped about 10:00 p.m. on a high bar. Loneliness crept in, but I was excited to be on my own. I did not think about it long and busied myself in setting up camp and preparing dinner. Soon after eating, I retired in full daylight of the midnight sun to the comfort of my new tent. I was tired. It had been a long and full day.

It was July 1. I was awakened in the morning by the grunt of an animal. My heart raced. A bear? I grabbed my shotgun and peered out the tent door. A cow moose ambled along the river. I relaxed. The noises I made scared the moose into the river and it continued across to the other shore. All was quiet again except for the faint murmur of the river and the overwhelming drone of mosquitoes. I got up and ate pancakes for breakfast. I then tested my shotgun. This I brought for bear protection. There were other alternatives but this seemed the best one for me. I had experience with shotguns but this meant making a commitment to keep the heavy gun with me at all times. If I didn't have it when I needed it, I might as well just leave it at home. I also secured long lines to the bow and stern of my canoe and did a number of other organizational things before leaving the site.

It was afternoon before I got back on the water. I paddled hard and reached Bettles by approximately 8:00 p.m. that evening. It had rained most of the afternoon and I approached the Bettles Ranger Station wet to the core and feeling like a drowned rat. Dave Price and Kathy Cook, visiting rangers from the Florida's Everglades National Park, were there. They invited me in to dry off and share a hot drink with them. That evening, in the warmth of the station, I enjoyed their good company. Dave and Kathy were soon to be flown to the upper Alatna River to begin a raptor survey as they descended the stream. Meeting Dave Price here was an amazing coincidence. Knowing I would have to work after the trip was finished, I had applied for a winter seasonal job in Everglades National Park before beginning the trip. I specifically applied for an Environmental Education position. Dave was supervisor of that program in the southern district. I expressed my interest in working for his program and he said he would take a close look at my application when he returned to Everglades. He could now place a person with the paperwork I submitted.[1]

Another visitor at the ranger station was Mike Kunz who was an archeologist for the Bureau of Land Management (BLM). This was another coincidence, though, I did not know it at the time. Mike has done several intense archeological surveys in Etivlik Lake in the National Petroleum Reserve Alaska, an area I would be traveling through on my journey. I immediately recognized that Etivlik Lake was an important archeological site when I arrived there but its specific significance would not be revealed to me until many years later.

Thick clouds filled the sky the next day. Rain came in brief, intense showers. It was 5:00 p.m. before I was again underway. The

---

[1] Dave Price hired me for an environmental education position that fall. He also hired Kristi Link as part of the team. Kristi and I became coworkers. We fell in love and were married in 1986.

Koyukuk was swollen and turbulent. We heard flash flood warnings on the radio for rivers of the area. I proceeded cautiously to the mouth of the John River. From here, I began to slowly make my way up that river. A shudder of apprehension went through my body when I became aware that I was also leaving behind my last touch with civilization for a long time. The freedom of being on my own and the thought of facing the unknown filled me with excitement. A wilderness spirit was taking hold in me—one of fright and joy mingled together. I could walk along the still exposed shorelines and gravel bars while tracking my canoe (pulling the canoe upstream with lines). The silty brown river was swift and wide. I often had to paddle hard into the current to reach suitable walking areas on the opposite shore. I moved tediously slow but at least it was forward progress.

The river meandered through thick spruce forest lowland. Clouds born on turbulent winds threatened rain but no rain fell. I proceeded upriver about 2 1/2 miles and camped on the bank above a large bar. I placed a marker at the water's edge. The river rose two inches while I ate dinner. I made a quick calculation and figured at that rate, the river would rise almost three feet by morning. My calculations were correct. The next morning, I woke up to find the shorelines and bars completely inundated. When planning the trip, I had

hoped not to find the John or Alatna Rivers in this condition. Moving upriver effectively depended on there being exposed shorelines and bars. Now I knew things would be much tougher.

I inched along the shoreline pulling my canoe and feeling my way walking in the silty water. It was cold and deep, chest-high on occasions. Sometimes I struggled through the shoreline brush and to get around fallen trees that blocked my path. I scrambled up and down banks. When travel was no longer possible on one side of the river, I had to get in the canoe and paddle hard to reach the other side. The current always swept me downstream from where I started, a distance I had to regain. Paddling was sometimes effective but most of the time, I spent walking in the cold, swift water. At the end of an exhausting day, I had gained only six miles. The sky was clearing, however, and by late afternoon I noticed that the river was already dropping.

The river dropped as fast as it rose. By morning, the shorelines and gravel bars were reappearing. It was the Fourth of July. The sun shone brightly. The silt swirling in the river radiated a pearly sheen. I was a long way from firecrackers, Fourth of July celebrations, and gatherings of people. I thought of people I missed and things that were important to me. I had a lot of time to think as I worked my way upriver.

The pace was faster now that the river was lower. Two Canada geese lifted off a gravel bar and flew downriver. Bohemian waxwings fluttered back and forth over the river channel in maneuvers to catch insects on the wing. Semipalmated plovers guarded their gravel bar territories with piercing calls. I gained 12 additional miles up the big river and reached the mouth of the Malamute Fork of the John River. This stream was much smaller and shallower than the John.

Tracking my canoe up the Malamute Fork for a day and a half brought me to my first portage. There before me was a 45-degree slope covered with dense alder, willow, and spruce. The vegetation was so thick that it would hardly allow a person to pass. I made three trips up that incline, the first two carrying a heavy pack. On the final trip, I took the canoe; one hand

5

hanging onto the bow thwart, the other grabbing alder branches for support and pulling leverage. If I had let the canoe go, it would have crashed to the bottom of the slope. The canoe's lightness was now evident and appreciated. I was able to tie it off to alder branches occasionally, which allowed me to take rests and change pulling positions. In this manner, I moved up the 300-foot incline to where the gradient slacked off and the vegetation thinned. The rest of the portage was much easier. I camped near a dry ridge that was a major game trail. I could hear a winnowing snipe performing its mating display. The afternoon was warm and the air thick with insects. Mosquitoes, horseflies, black flies, deer flies, and houseflies came in swarms. Little could be heard in the afternoon quiet except the buzzing of insects.

I completed the portage the following day. It led to an indistinct tributary of the East Fork of Henshaw Creek. This stream had promise at first. It was narrow, deep, and lined with grassy banks. But it soon changed character. Willows closed in and choked off the channel except where beaver activity kept the channel open. Progress downriver became painfully slow. I crashed, jerked, and pulled my way through willows—their drowned, lower branches scraping my shins. Rain coated the upper branches which grew well over my head.

I was soaked as I passed through them. I sometimes stepped in holes and went up to my neck in the frigid water. A scene from the movie *African Queen* came to mind—Bogart and Hepburn pulling their boat through a jungle river. There were no leeches in this water, at least not big ones, just swarms of vicious mosquitoes around my head. At times the willows were so thick that it was not possible to move through them. I was forced to portage. Portaging was no easier. The valley was a tangle of willow and dwarf birch, spongy wet vegetation, and mud covered the ground. I had to make three trips to move all my gear. It took hours to go less than a mile. Lesser yellowlegs protested my presence. They heaped their insults on my misery with their loud piercing and repetitive calls. The area they protected seemed to go for miles. When portaging, I was forced to travel through one area five times and each time, I was escorted by one of these birds. They harassed me continuously.

I was worried about bears in this valley but did not see any. Moose were plentiful. They seemed very startled to see me. Two days of struggling through this valley and I was nearing a tributary that came in from the north. Moving up this stream would lead me to the Alatna River drainage. I went right by the tributary. It was so choked with willows, it blended perfectly with the shoreline. I climbed out of the willow quagmire of the river channel to higher ground. A beautiful valley unfolded before me covered with cotton grass tundra. I pulled out my compass and triangulated on several peaks that rose predominately above the valley to pinpoint my position.

I moved back upstream for about a mile. From a significant hill, I recognized the northern tributary by the willow line that outlined its meandering course down the valley. It was totally impassible by canoe and I prepared to portage. I felt elated that my path was clearly before me now, even though I faced the drudgery of portaging. To reduce this drudgery, I needed to complete the portage in two trips. I decided to drag the canoe overland with some gear in it while carrying the smaller food pack on my back. This would allow me to carry the heavier, bulkier equipment pack by itself. My concern about bears prompted me to tote my eight-pound shotgun on all trips back and forth.

The next two and a half days were miserable. Four miles of open and expansive country separated me and the next place I could float my canoe. The land looked gentle and serene with a nearly continuous

carpet of the white flower-like seed stalks of cotton grass. But the white carpet belied the mass of stems clumped together at the base of each cotton grass plant into a structure known as a tussock.

Each step across this land was agony—a test of endurance, agility, and patience. Tussocks are made up of living and dead stems and can be hundreds of years old. They bend and sway when stepped on, sending a person pitching in a random direction. In this country, tussocks are packed close together and build up to three feet above the ground. It is like trying to walk on basketballs.

I trudged through them, one laborious step at a time, often crashing to the ground as tussocks gave way under foot. Mosquitoes and horseflies hounded me all the way. Carrying the unwieldy equipment pack or dragging the canoe through shrubbery and wet tussock tundra was excruciating. I sweated in the hot sun and collapsed in exhaustion after each spurt of forward movement.

Traveling through the valley had its rewards. The cottony seed balls springing from the tussocks covered the valley floor and provided a pleasant foreground against a backdrop of the surrounding peaks. Moose were plentiful. I saw two large bulls and six cows the first day. Waterfowl and shorebirds were also plentiful, including, much to my dismay, yellowlegs. I was exhausted and evenings were uncomfortable because I had to camp in and around tussocks, but I had a front row seat as moose passed close to my camp in the morning. I did not encounter bears in the valley and sign of their presence was rare.

The valley was peaceful, free from all human activity but my most prominent memories—my main impression of my time there—was the pain of traveling through it. I was ecstatic when

I reached a small but open creek from the mountains that signaled I had crossed a low divide and was in the Alatna River drainage. The tussock portaging was over. After a long rest and refreshingly long drink of

water, I continued down this creek which had no name but would eventually run into Bedrock Creek. After a while, the willows closed in and my heart sank. But soon it opened up again and with the flow of additional tributaries into the creek, it grew wider and stronger. I pushed hard to reach Bedrock Creek. I knew that once I reached this stream, it was clear sailing. While planning the trip, I had studied these drainages on false-color infrared aerial photographs and Bedrock Creek appeared open and distinct. I reached Bedrock Creek and continued down that stream for a few more miles before camping. I was glad to put the tussocks and willow-clogged creeks behind me.

Bedrock Creek was of different character than the narrow-channeled tributary I had been traveling on. The creek became slower and wider with more open gravel bars along the shore and shallow, gravel riffles in the channel. It had to be walked most of the way in this upper section. It abounded with grayling, whitefish, and suckers. The longnose sucker (*Catostomus catostomus*) is the

only sucker species found in Alaska. I camped on a prominent bar on a sharp turn in the river. A moose visited me soon after I climbed into my tent. It startled me; I was still edgy about bears. But there was

9

no sign of bears. I saw fresh wolf tracks earlier in the day. Wildlife was near but often not visible.

The next morning, I enjoyed a leisurely breakfast under a warm sun and took a bath in the stream. I also repaired some equipment and so got a later start. I tracked and paddled hard to reach the Malamute Fork of the Alatna. Bedrock Creek became wider and deeper and soon lining was not required. I reached the Malamute Fork by late evening. This was a beautiful stream, a hidden gem south of the Brooks Range. It was wide and flowed clear. It had large, clean gravel bars providing grand views of the prominent peaks in the area, particularly Heart Mountain and the jagged Deadman Mountain. Its valley teemed with bird life.

I drifted a few miles down the river in the peaceful evening atmosphere. Massive thunderheads formed mountains in the sky to the east, illuminated by the low sun. They glowed white and golden, with touches of alpenglow along their lower edges. I was about ready to camp but spotted a grizzly bear ambling along the right shore. The bear had thick yellow-gold fur. It looked fleetingly back at me, climbed the bank, and disappeared into some trees. I then paddled upstream a short distance and set up camp on the opposite shore. After dinner I walked along the gravel bar as the sun was nearing the horizon. The thunderheads had spread out and become less distinct. All was bathed in a golden-red light. All was tranquil. I watched for a few moments the place where the bear had disappeared. No movement. I returned to my tent. I took in the sun, sky, and river for a while longer and went to bed.

It was sunny and warm on this July 13 morning. The mosquitoes were outrageous. I was anxious to get on the river and move. I paddled hard but still took the time to appreciate the beauty unfolding before me. The river thrived with life in its summer opulence. Shortly after starting off, I came upon nesting bald eagles. The nest was close to the river in the broken top of a ragged spruce tree. The birds left their nest and circled, uttering their forced and feeble alarm calls in irritation. I got the message. One chick could be seen in the nest from my vantage point. Its head moved back and forth

as it watched the action. Shorebirds populated the shoreline— semipalmated plovers, sandpipers, and yellowlegs. Ducks, gulls, and mergansers were common. Further downriver I saw an osprey glide over the river. At other times during the day, I came upon a Canada goose family of two adults and seven goslings, a great horned owl, and a marsh hawk. A black-tailed cross fox (color variant of the red fox *Vulpes vulpes*) hunted along the shore, probably looking for young birds or eggs. The clear waters of the river were

rich in aquatic life. I flyfished for grayling in the still water among tall, arching spruce-tree sweepers. The surrounding scenery was mirrored perfectly on the smooth river surface.

I passed the mouth of the Iniakuk River. It is the outlet of Iniakuk Lake to the north. Between this and Tobuk Creek was some

wreckage at the base of a small shoreline bluff. Parts of an aircraft were strewn about and battered from a crash and from several spring breakups. The plane appeared to be a single engine Otter or Beaver. As I continued downriver, I saw several more pieces of the plane scattered on the river bottom: a door, a tail section, part of the fuselage. I was later told the pilot of the plane had tried to take off from the river, didn't get high enough, and crashed into the bluff.

With a tired, sore back, I paddled into the evening. I was not sure exactly where I was on the river, but wanted to get as close to the Alatna as possible. It had been a long and full day. I rounded a bend and before me was the wide expanse of river. Surprised and weary, I slipped from the clear water of the Malamute Fork into the silty waters of the Alatna. A common loon greeted me. Here was my pathway into the heart of the Brooks Range. Because of scouring from continental glaciation that ended about 12,000 years ago, the major rivers of the Brooks Range meander through wide, U-shaped valleys. This meandering is most pronounced in the middle and lower portions of these rivers, the area on the Alatna where I was to begin my upstream journey.

Though happy to reach the Alatna, I felt a bit let down at viewing this low-lying country where the river bars and shorelines were muddy and unappealing. The beautiful river I had just experienced was still fresh in my memory. I paddled to the opposite shore and began tracking my canoe upriver.

I had reached a critical point on my trip. I had been out two weeks and my body was now depending almost entirely on the food I had brought with me. A tooth had begun to hurt and was causing me concern. I now faced 180 miles of upstream travel and from there, the trip would pass through some of the most remote country I have ever been in. There would be no turning back. I was lonely, missing friends

and family. My mind swam through past love affairs, music that I enjoyed, certain foods, and routines—those things that I identified with civilization and was now without.

A bottle of suntan lotion turned up missing and I was angry. The lotion was necessary in the intense arctic sunlight, but its scent had also brought back memories of a good Hawaiian vacation I had with a close friend. Must we throw away our past on a trip like this? Should our relationship with God or the power within us take the place of human relationships? I thought not. Though, to dwell on these presently missing aspects of my life would not be good either. There would be time for friends and family and to enjoy old amenities. I just needed to get back safely. Now was the time I had committed to be alone. I had the option to continue down the Alatna River to its junction with the Koyukuk River at Allakaket, then fly out from there and end the trip, but I knew I would not take that option. I would monitor my painful tooth as I continued upriver and keep thought and action aimed toward safety.

The suntan lotion was on the bottom of the canoe beneath the big pack. I was delighted to find it and embraced it as if it was a lost friend. It was indeed needed during the rest of the trip. The hot, sunny weather had just begun.

CHAPTER 2

The Alatna River and into Gates of the Arctic National Park

Nonnative exploration of the Noatak and Kobuk River basins did not occur until the 1880s. Lieutenant George M. Stoney, U.S. Navy, traveled up the Kobuk River to Cosmos Creek in 1884 where he built a fort and overwintered. From Ft. Cosmos he explored the Noatak, Selawik, Alatna, Coville, and Reed rivers. He even traveled overland to Point Barrow that winter. Lt. Stoney is credited for naming many features in the western Brooks Range.

Had the Alatna changed much since Stoney's exploration? My first camp on the river was an old burn site on top of a small bluff. It provided grand views up and down the river channel. Had those early explorers seen this very scene over 100 years ago? I could see that the site was used by wildlife to access the shoreline and the upland areas. Bear and moose tracks were predominant. I feasted on Malamute Fork grayling that evening while I watched the silent river flow.

That night a bear came into my camp. It knocked over the equipment pack, tossed around my boots, and bit into my life vest. It also batted around a small food bag and bit into that as well. My exhaustion was complete. I did not wake up. The bear miraculously avoided the pots I had placed on the large food pack and other equipment that would have collapsed with a clamor and sounded the alarm of its presence. I was shocked in the morning upon discovering my disorganized camp, but the bear left before it did any real damage and for this I was thankful.

It was a beautiful, sunny morning. Flowers were reaching their summer peak. Asters (*Aster sp.*), white camas (*Anticlea elegans*), wild chives (*Allium schoenoprasum*), wild sweet-pea (*Hedysarum mackenzii*), and two kinds of fireweed *(Epilobium sp.)* were in full bloom. Tracking the canoe upriver was good. I was able to walk along the exposed shore hardly missing a step most of the day. Changing sides was rarely necessary. Tracks of grizzly bear, black bear, and moose were visible in the shoreline mud, but I only saw one cow moose this day.

From the opposite shore, a great horned owl watched my slow progress upriver. A group of northern shrikes were chatting it up in the same general area. It may have been fledglings hounding the adults for food. Thunderheads built up all around me and a brief rainstorm passed over around noon. I made good time up the slow and meandering river.

Toward the end of the day, a colorful patch appeared upriver. As the patch approached, it took on shape, and I was able to distinguish it as a red-and-white Folbot, a type of collapsible kayak, with two paddlers dripping  their double-bladed paddles in unison. The paddlers were the two visiting rangers from Everglades National Park I had met in Bettles. Dave Price and Kathy Cook were using their vacation time to do a volunteer peregrine falcon study for Gates of the Arctic National

Park. I was very happy to see them. It had been over two weeks since I had any human contact. We talked a long while, exchanging adventures and what we had encountered on our journeys. They had some bear trouble and pointed out the location of the incident on my map. We departed; they proceeded toward their pickup point and I, reluctant to give up any forward gain, continued my upstream progress.

The shoreline and mud bars had changed in character. They now consisted of mud and loosely packed sand. I sunk in deep with each step. Walking became tedious and exhausting. I tried paddling against the current and found I could make progress by keeping close to shore and using slower areas in the current.

It was getting late in the evening but mountains loomed directly ahead of me. A peak on the right had a great white slash diagonally across its southern slope. Snow and ice were packed in a steep creek channel.

I pushed on and soon found myself flanked by those mountains. I had entered the Brooks Range. The geology of the Brooks Range is complicated. Around 190 million years ago, there was a large ocean body called the Canada Basin. A great rift, or pulling apart, of the sea floor caused the Arctic Alaska Terrane which was attached to what became the Arctic Islands in Canada to split away and be rotated south. Rocks in this terrane were a package of Precambrian basement rocks and younger sedimentary rocks. This buttress of hard rock forced a pileup of north-drifting oceanic fragments and terranes, culminating 140 million years ago in the formation of the Brooks Range.

I found a mound of sand isolated from the shore by a dry channel. Here I set up my camp. From the height of the mound, I could look downriver upon the smooth surface and see the reflection of the mountains I had become a part of.

The next two days I was able to paddle against the current. Despite what seemed a tediously slow pace, I made reasonably good progress. The river radically meandered back and forth in its wide, glaciated valley and I often faced strong west winds as the river turned and flowed southeast and east. One evening, a tremendous wind came roaring down the valley, picking up clouds of dust off the bars and turning the river into a mass of whitecaps. My forward progress was immediately halted. I angled my canoe to reach an island across the river. I set up camp and waited out a heavy rainstorm that followed the wind. It passed as quickly as it had blown in. The golden sun came out and it was calm again.

I was close to the Gates of the Arctic National Park boundary. The park got its name from wilderness advocate Robert Marshall. He had traveled the North Fork of the Koyukuk River country, which is now included in the park, frequently from 1929 to 1939. Marshall was struck by two opposite peaks along that stream called Frigid Crags and Boreal Mountain that for him looked like a gateway from Alaska's central Brooks Range into the far arctic north. He coined the term Gates of the Arctic for this location, a name that was eventually applied to the new park when it was created in 1980.

On July 16, near the park boundary, I encountered another paddler moving downriver. Miraculously it was another friend. I had met Doug Smith at Isle

Royale National Park four years earlier where he was doing wolf research on the island under the direction of Dr. Rolf Peterson. I was a seasonal park ranger at the time. Tall, young, and athletic, Doug was doing his first solo canoe trip in grizzly bear country. He began his adventure after being flown into Takahula Lake.[2] Despite his reservations about paddling in bear country, he was presently shirtless and shoeless, enjoying a leisurely float downstream. We had lunch together on a gravel bar and talked about mutual friends and old times, the philosophy of solo paddling, plans, and trips we might do in the future. Four hours passed quickly. The hour was getting late and we had to go our separate ways. We left with the feeling that perhaps we would do a major canoe trip together someday.

I traveled late into the midnight sun, looking for a suitable campsite. During this time, I thought much about the things that Doug and I had discussed. Finally, a good place appeared. I camped at the mouth of Takahula River—the first night inside of Gates of the Arctic National Park and Preserve. This park was one of ten new Alaska park areas created along with the expansion of three original park areas in Alaska with the signing of the Alaska National Interest Lands Conservation Act (ANILCA) by President Jimmy Carter on December 2, 1980. Gates was billed as the premier wilderness park in the country and contains 7,167,192 acres of designated wilderness plus six wild and scenic rivers.[3] I will be travelling on three of those rivers on my journey—the John, Alatna, and the Noatak. ANILCA more than doubled the size of National Park

---

[2] Dr. Douglas W. Smith is now the Senior Wildlife Biologist for Yellowstone National Park. He is the Project Leader for the Yellowstone Wolf Project and oversees the reintroduction of wolves back into Yellowstone which began in 1995.

[3] The six wild and scenic rivers in the park are the Noatak, Kobuk, Alatna, John, Tinayguk, and the North Fork of the Koyukuk.

Service acres and protected 43, 583, 000 acres of NPS administered land in Alaska.

The Alatna bent sharply southward at my campsite location. I could see more than two miles downriver. The sun flooded the valley and jagged mountains shown with red-orange light. They seemed very close. I was exhausted but very happy that I had reached a good campsite and the scene before me was magnificent.

The next day (July 17) was clear and hot. The cumulus clouds had vanished. The sun beat down on me unmercifully. It drained my energy and I moved lethargically through the afternoon. The river was changing, becoming narrow and swift. Its waters were clearing. River bars and shorelines now consisted of more gravel and walking on them was easier. Paddling against the current became difficult and I resorted to tracking my canoe once again.

I made a side trip into Takahula Lake. Resting in its mountain-rimmed valley, the lake's deep blue waters shimmered in the hazy heat. Dragonflies patrolled the airspace for insects. Flies and bees buzzed to and fro in  search of nectar-rich flowers. Fish lazily fed on the surface. I enjoyed a moment of rest by the still lake then returned to the river.

Continuing upstream, I passed a large ice wedge in a cut bank. The ice was melting rapidly because of the hot temperature, which I guessed was in the mid-90s. This caused huge chunks of the bank to tumble into the river. The permafrost—permanently frozen ground produced by the cold climatic conditions in the arctic—was melting before my eyes. I never expected the temperature in the arctic to be this hot. Was this the effect of human-induced global warming? When I worked for Gates of the Arctic NPP in 1982, there was a postdoctoral researcher named Ann Odaz who was studying the movement of the arctic treeline. The arctic treeline is the northern and altitudinal limit beyond which the climate is too harsh for trees to grow. It is the boundary between tundra and boreal forest. She was documenting how the "line" was moving farther north and higher up the mountain slopes because of warming temperatures in the arctic. That evening I did not feel well. I attributed this to prolonged exposure to the unrelenting sun and heat. I was hoping for a break from the intense sun the next day.

I felt exhausted the following morning. It was cooler with some high clouds in the sky. There was a cabin across from my camp owned by Bernd Gaedeke and I investigated it before continuing upriver. The well-built structure had enough good reading material to last an arctic winter. Some of the heftier books present included the *Iliad and Odyssey* by Homer, *Canterbury Tales* by Geoffrey Chaucer, *War and Peace* by Tolstoy, *Hawaii* by James Michener. And *Shardik* by Richard Adams, the book I was currently reading. I was not the only one to think this book was appropriate reading while in this country. Wildlife was not common. I saw one black bear and an occasional moose during the last few days. In the still morning, arctic terns hunted small fish in the shallows. Arctic terns live in perpetual summer, going from polar region to polar region. They are the marathoners of the migratory bird world, spending our winter months in the sea-ice zone of East Antarctica where it is summer. The ubiquitous and nonmigratory Canada jays have been my guardians for this upriver journey.

The Alatna River cuts through the Endicott Mountains[4] which are located in the middle of the Brooks Range and run some 151 miles east to west. They are bordered on the west by the Schwatka

---

[4] The Endicott Mountains were named in 1885 by Lt. A.T. Allen for William Crownishield Enidcott, US Secretary of War under President Grover Cleveland.

Mountains.[5] Notable formations in the Endicotts in this area are the upper Devonian sedimentary rocks of the Hunt Fork Shale and the Kanayuk Conglomerate. The latter is a fluvial deposit made by a river in its flood plain and can be up to 8,000 feet thick. It is believed to have formed a huge delta almost 500 miles long and 30 miles wide. I passed the Arrigetch Peaks late in the afternoon. These granitic formations intruded into the overlying Hunt Fork Shale over 90 million years ago. They have long been a landmark to the inland Inupiat of northwestern Alaska and the word 'Arrigetch' means "fingers of the hand extended." The bearing of these granite spires and their deep U-shaped valleys was overwhelming despite viewing them from a distance of eight miles. The Arrigetch Peaks attract mountain climbers from around the world. Most people access the area by flying into Circle Lake, a long oxbow of the main river just upstream from the Arrigetch Creek mouth. The area was showing signs of concentrated use because of its popularity. I came upon a wide fire ring with partially burnt tree trunks scattered around it. The fire created by these trees must have been huge. Footprints indicated a large group had camped there.

This fragile country cannot withstand excessive use without showing the scars of degradation. Undesignated campsites and trails have developed in the area. Problem bears have also moved in to take advantage of the new  food supply people bring in. There is so much more of the Brooks

[5] The Schwatka Mountains were named in 1884 by Lieutenant G. M. Stoney, U.S. Navy (USN), presumably for Lieutenant Frederick Schwatka, who had made a military reconnaissance along the Yukon River the previous year.

Range to explore that I wanted to avoid this human-trampled area and I did not need to deal with bears that had lost their fear of humans. I continued on to the mouth of the Kutuk River. Its wide, gravel delta provided an excellent campsite with unobstructed views of the river valley and surrounding mountains. A well-constructed subsistence cabin stood high on a wooded slope on the opposite bank. This location provided a fine vantage point downriver. The proprietor left a not-so-friendly note on the door—"Private Residence, Keep Out." The owner is considered a local rural resident, which is defined as a resident of a community or area adjacent to the park who are allowed to practice subsistence hunting and trapping in the National Park. It is a provision in ANILCA to allow Native Americans to continue their subsistence lifestyle which they have practiced for thousands of years. But the designation does not excluded non-natives. All rural residents who live in the subsistence-permitted area are allowed to practice subsistence in the National Park.

The character of the landscape changed dramatically during the next three days of ascending the Alatna. The river channel narrowed and became more braided. The river gradient increased rapidly to a 50-foot per mile drop. The river flowed colder, clearer, and swifter. Large rocks and gravel riffles increasingly broke the river's flow into churning white water. Mountains rose steeply in sweeping arcs from both sides of the channel. The swiftness of the water made for tough going today. My hands suffered as I hauled the boat upstream using the narrow painter line.

The weather remained dry with only high, thin clouds occasionally interrupting the clear blue sky. For this

I was thankful. Cool breezes blew down the valley most of the day. Nights were cooling down also as the sun slipped behind the mountains for a few hours before emerging again. I woke up to ice in my drinking cup and frost on the  ground on the morning of July 21. I heard varied thrushes singing. The vegetation was also changing. The dense spruce forest that filled the valleys and extended up the northwest facing slope had begun to thin.

On this day, I reached the arctic treeline! The spruce forests in the valley and on the slopes abruptly ended. I would not see spruce trees again until 23 days later along the Noatak River. I camped on arctic tundra for the first time this evening. The site was near a turnoff where a short distance to the SW is the Continental Divide. Over the divide in the same direction is Portage Creek that flows into the Noatak River. This route was used by the Inupiat and Nunatamiut hunters as a shortcut between the Alatna and the Noatak River basins. Wildlife sightings were scarce but tracks of moose, bear, and especially wolf, indicated that these animals were present and regularly using the area but keeping out of my sight.

The going was tougher now. Large rocks forced me away from the shoreline and into the river. In the numbing cold water, I pulled my canoe against the strong current, directing it around obstacles and trying to keep my balance on slippery, irregular boulders.

On the afternoon of the 22, two days before reaching the headwaters, I started a frustrating struggle upriver. Ahead, perhaps 150 yards, my eyes caught movement. Three wolves materialized. They spread out in a radiating pattern generally moving in my direction. The first wolf was black and ran parallel to the river channel.

It was gone in an instant. The second tawny wolf ran diagonally up slope and soon disappeared. The third wolf appeared tan-gray in the distance and proceeded straight up the mountainside. It took several minutes before finding topography that would conceal it. I excitedly maneuvered for more glimpses of the wolves but did not see them again. I stayed in the area to eat lunch and to keep a lookout for more wildlife to appear.

Soon after continuing, I saw a large grizzly bear walking on the slope above me. It had no interest in me at all and continued down the valley. I made slow progress that day. Not long after seeing the

bear, I came upon a large expanse of ice spread out on both sides of the river. The dripping water from its rapidly melting surface sounded like a waterfall. The ice was cooling the surrounding air. Its interior glowed deep blue. The ice built up over the winter as the main river channel became constricted during freeze-up. The continuous flow of the river forced water out of the channel and onto flood plain. Layer after layer of ice was deposited. Much of the ice will melt away during the summer but it is likely that some will remain before the cold weather returns. The ice

I am observing may be from multiple years. It is called *aufeis* (pronounced "off ice") which is German for "ice on top." The meltwater provided good growing conditions for wildflowers, particularly dwarf fireweed.

Not far from this ice sheet, I reached the Weyahok River, a major tributary of the Alatna. It carried two thirds of the river's volume. The confluence of the two streams provided another rich habitat for wildflowers. Past this tributary, the Alatna became extremely shallow and in most places did not float my canoe. I lugged and jerked the canoe over small rocks and took advantage of any semblance of a channel. The water numbed my feet and the cool north wind chilled me even more. Arctic warblers defensively protected their willow shelters along the river. This old-world species has come a long way to breed in the arctic. It commonly winters in the Philippines. Cold and tired, I could go no farther even though the headwater lakes were very close now. I camped near a trickling mountain stream, trying to stay protected from the wind behind its cut bank. My stove was malfunctioning and little wood was around to build a fire. It took 25 minutes to boil water, but finally I was able to get my meal together.

I felt better after dinner. I noticed movement in the dim light. It was a group of 12 caribou that had just come out the pass to the west. They moved north and east, stopping often to feed and look over at me. As a group, their movements appeared uneven—walking, running in short spurts, stopping to feed, and looking up to surveil the landscape. They would bunch up or split into small groups and spread out only to come together again, but they were always on the move in one general direction. I watched them off and on for about 20 minutes. The group contained three or four large bulls, several cows and a few young calves. The dominant bull led the herd into a valley east of the river, and they gradually disappeared from my sight.

Early the following morning, a sound filtered into my consciousness—a slow mournful cry, building in intensity and rising in scale. It suddenly brought me out of sleep. A wolf was howling. I stirred with excitement and thought of getting up and looking for wolves. I laid and listened but soon fell back into a deep sleep that lasted late into the morning.

CHAPTER 3

The Headwaters and Survey Pass

It is July 23. I am stiff and sore when I get up. Everything is in disarray. The keel of the canoe is showing much wear. The day is hard on it. The river, little more than a shallow creek now, deceives me and I take a channel that dries up. From a hill, I can see the way back to the river, but there are no headwater lakes in sight. I shuttle

the canoe and equipment back to the main channel and continue on. The river begins to deepen and it widens out but soon becomes sedge-choked. I am encouraged despite getting bogged down in the vegetation. This is what an outlet to a lake looks like. Soon a channel clears and I punch through to open water, gliding on the calm surface of a lake. I have made it to the headwaters of the Alatna River.

I am not alone. A National Outdoor Leadership School (NOLS) group is setting up camp on the south end. Two loads of people are brought in by a Beaver bush plane with pontoons. Fifteen make up the party. I paddle towards a cabin, which is highly visible in the northeast end of the lake. The cabin is owned by Bernd Gaedeke. I had prearranged to have a resupply of food dropped off here. Bernd would be bringing it in during one of his many flights to the cabin. I expected this to cost some money but Bernd was happy to do it for free.

Two people from Massachusetts and their guide were at the cabin. Bernd had flown them up from his lodge at Iniakuk Lake to view migrating caribou. Jesse Hunt, the guide, was originally from Fremont, Michigan, but had spent a lot of time in the Wrangle Mountains in southcentral Alaska. He said he was part Chippewa Indian. He had spent six winter months alone in a cabin. It drove him crazy once but he stayed and trapped. Once he had followed a wolf shot by aerial hunters late into the night but could not catch up to it. He started to fear for his own life as the wolf led him farther into the cold. Finally, he had had enough and turned back. The next day he found the wolf curled up under a large spruce tree. It had died alone, still free. The northern lights shone that night. His respect for the animal held no bounds. He had many stories and we talked a long time together about philosophy, spiritual matters, touching the land, and being alone.

Earlier, a NOLS instructor named Leslie paid us a visit. This was the first trip this organization was attempting in this area. They have a branch in Palmer, northeast of Anchorage. The group is going to do day trips out of the headwater lakes area, then backpack down the Alatna, eventually crossing a pass to the Noatak River where they will pick up Kleppers (collapsible kayaks) that had been flown in. With these they will float down the Noatak to Noatak Village where they will fly out to Kotzebue. This is an ambitious trip with people who have little experience in the Arctic.

27

Bernd came in late in the day. I got to meet this generous and gracious man. He had brought in my resupply of food, except the margarine and cheese that Jeff Chapman was keeping refrigerated but had not delivered to Bernd in Fairbanks. We discussed how to get that food to me when Bernd received it. He was willing to fly into another lake along my route to drop it off. In the meantime, Bernd encouraged me to stay at his cabin and rest. He flew off, taking his guests and guide back to the lodge.

Clouds were present all day, but the sun shone through many times. The wind was fickle: gusting at times and calm at others. The mosquitoes were bad in the stillness of the evening. Fish! The lower Alatna seemed barren of fish, but the upper, shallow reaches, especially the lake outlet, abounded with fish—grayling, round whitefish, and possibly char. They dimpled the lake surface as soon as the wind died down. I found stoneflies, Chironomids (midges), black flies, and caddisflies, among the streambed rocks.

I stayed at Bernd's cabin for three days. These were the first rest days of the trip. Though it was a rest for my body, I wasn't idle. The time was spent busily repairing my stove which I got working as well as it ever had, sewing up the crotch of my pants that had split due to the strain on the seams of moving up river, and packing the new food. I also take time to fish for grayling, take a bath, wash some clothes, study maps, and read the book *Shardik* by Richard Adams.

By the second day, I had cleaned the place and was prepared to leave in the morning. Morning came and as I was departing, Bernd's plane roared in. He brought my margarine and cheese. In addition, he brought homemade English muffins, a loaf of homemade wheat bread, real butter, and assorted fruits that his wife Pat had prepared for me. There was more. Bernd, noticing the wear on the bottom of my canoe, purchased fiberglass and resin when he was in Fairbanks and brought it to me on this flight to the cabin so I could patch up the canoe before hitting the trail again. I was astonished at this display of northern hospitality.

Bernd empathized with my trip. In his youth, he had crossed the Brooks Range on foot, attempting to live off the land. He had some harrowing experiences, including the loss of his movie camera when trying to cross a swollen stream. Even considering this, his generosity was way beyond any expectation. What was even more surprising is that he knew I had worked for the National Park Service (NPS) in past years. He passionately hated the Park Service. He lost part of his hunting guide area when Gates of the Arctic National Park was created in 1980. This was bad enough but from the time NPS took over as land manager, he felt its eyes on him. He accused park staff of spying on him, watching his activities using spotting scopes and from the air. He felt the NPS coveted his property on the Alatna River. He would take this hatred to the grave.

I repaired the canoe as best I could, laying the resin-soaked fiberglass along the keel of the canoe. It wasn't a pretty job, but I hoped that the extra layers might prevent the bottom from wearing through completely should I have any more canoe dragging over rocks to do. It turned out the damage already inflicted on the canoe was only the beginning and there would be much hard work and worry ahead.

The instructions said the resin needed 8-24 hours to dry. I had to stay at Bernd's another day. After canoe repairs and packing the remainder of my food, I truly had a day of rest. I lounged around, took a short hike, slept, and read. I saw several American pipits and Savannah sparrow around the cabin and a female harlequin duck with three chicks near the lake outlet. Later in the day, Bernd returned, bringing with him a party that had just floated the Killik River. Their guide was Bill McAfee. He was a slender man. His face was darkly tan and his manner was relaxed. Bill has been all over the Brooks Range. Between trips for Bernd, he hikes up and down side canyons of the major river drainages. Bill also guides in Idaho and has led fishing trips in the South American Andes where he has also done some fisheries biology work. He received his master's degree in Fisheries Biology at the University of Michigan.

Bernd had dinner at the cabin before taking his guests back to the lodge. He filled my ear with his trials and tribulations with the Park Service. His operation seemed consistent with park values. The grounds were immaculate; his workmanship was meticulous. Bears or other animals were not attracted to, nor could they penetrate, Bernd's well-built cabins. There was nothing the Park Service should have been concerned about. Yet Bernd was convinced he was being harassed. It was an uncomfortable position for me. I had worked for Gates of the Arctic only three years earlier but had not detected any feeling that Bernd was singled out as a troublemaker. In fact, many of the people I had worked for respected him. They thought of him as one of a dying breed of Alaskans—a hardworking, self-made man, extremely knowledgeable of the land, generous, and hospitable. But they were certainly aware of his stubbornness. I thought that Bernd and the Park Service could have had a good partnership had there not been so much misunderstanding and distrust.

Bernd took off, leaving Bill to get ready to take a group down the Nigu River. We talked into the night over a dinner of Spam, instant potatoes, corn, and Jell-O cheesecake. In the morning, Bill and I enjoyed a wonderful breakfast of cheese omelets with real eggs. We also ate Pat's homemade English muffins, and drank cowboy coffee (coffee made by boiling fresh grounds). Bill then helped me make the portage to the second headwater lake. I dragged the canoe over the tundra with a rope around my waist and a food bag inside. He took the large heavy pack. I said goodbye to a new friend and indicated that I might visit him next winter at his home in Bradenton, Florida. I was on my way again.[6]

---

[6] Bernd Gaedeke and Bill McAfee died in an airplane crash on August 8, 1991, when Bernd was attempting to depart Amilchiak Lake in his 185 Cessna with Bill aboard. The plane lifted off the water, turned, and took a nosedive into the lake. Bernd's wife, Pat, sought a better relationship with the NPS, anxious for years of the bad feelings and suspicion to end.

CHAPTER 4

Crossing the Divide

It was a short portage to the third lake. Caribou had been through here by the thousands. Their parallel trails were dug deep into the mud as if someone had dragged a giant rake across the landscape. A thick mat of hair was washed up along the windblown shoreline. This is a major migration route used by the Western Arctic Caribou Herd (WAH). The WAH is one of the largest caribou herds in the world with over 200,000 individuals. Caribou in the WAH undertake one of the longest, intact migrations of any terrestrial mammal in the world. They head for their calving ground in the spring which is described as the heart of the herd. The WAH calving ground is located near the Utukok River Uplands

in the National Petroleum Reserve Alaska. Nearly every caribou that belongs to the WAH is born here. I saw a few caribou stragglers but no large herds.

Beyond the third lake was another small, narrow lake. Beyond this I stood on the Continental Divide. This was Survey Pass, a major landmark on my trip. It had been a long struggle to get here. I felt a surge of pride and happiness as I gazed across this low-lying pass with open vistas north toward the Nigu and Killik Rivers and south toward the Alatna River. This is where I wanted to be, the place that looked so intriguing on the map. But the space! I was standing in a vast tundra plain and feeling quite alone.

Traveling now would be downhill, downstream, and at least for a short distance, down the North Slope of the Brooks Range. I moved to a lake on the other side of the divide then found a willow-filled drainage leading to another lake two miles to the northwest. It had an outlet to a small lake that led to the Nigu River. Dragging the canoe and carrying the large packs took its toll. This portage was about two miles, the longest of the trip. Yet the open tundra was much easier to traverse than the brush-choked valleys to the south. I saw a golden eagle and two parasitic jaegers during the day but little other wildlife. The long, arduous day ended with a rewarding campsite beside the lake. The sun went down and the wind turned chilly.

It was warm, sunny, and calm in the morning. It is July 28. The creek was all that stirred in the quiet except for a willow ptarmigan family that walked through my camp. I moved out of the lake into the outlet which had enough flow to carry my canoe. The slow-flowing stream teemed with aquatic life. Two lake trout over 20 inches torpedoed by and several large grayling were frantic for a place to hide. Bottom rocks were covered with algae, rich food for aquatic insects. The outlet probably flows all year long, like a spring, even in the dead of winter. Such a stable environment is rare in the arctic and provides much better living condition for aquatic organisms. Subject to neither flood nor drying up, production can go on uninterrupted. Robins abound in the tall willows near the creek.

The outlet creek flowed into an unnamed creek that eventually took me into the Nigu River. I was never sure exactly when that happened because the two streams braided together with many channels. The Nigu valley opened up. A luxuriant blanket of green filled the lowland, vibrant against the blue sky, glowing with the summer sun. Barren and sharp-edged mountains rose up on each side. The clear air made them seem close enough to touch. All this space, but no wildlife was in sight. I scanned the countryside carefully. Farther downriver I was jolted into reality. Wildlife was present. There, at my feet, was a perfect set of grizzly bear tracks imprinted in the river mud. They were no older than this morning.

Paddling under a high bank, I had an urge to stop. Intuitively, I felt something was up on the bluff. I left the canoe and scrambled up the bank onto a flat plane. I scanned the landscape and to my left was something brown. A cub grizzly? I studied it with binoculars. To my joy and surprise, it was a wolf. We stared at each other for a while, then it began to trot in a wide circle around me. I am always amazed that wolves can trot over uneven and rough terrain, while fixing their gaze on you with no need to look down or forward. It was trying to get downwind of me. After it caught my scent, the wolf turned and headed for a nearby ridge. It stopped to look at me many times but finally disappeared over the ridge accompanied by two long-tailed jaegers that harassed it all the way. I thought it was gone, but when I looked back in that direction, I could just make out the wolf's ears and face. It was peering over the ridge for one last look at me. I returned to the canoe and moved on. Besides this wolf, I saw eight caribou stragglers this day, mostly single cows or cows with a calf.

The river was shallow and obstinate. Many riffles forced me out of the canoe to drag it over the rocks. A strong headwind made paddling in deep areas no fun either. The chilly breeze cooled much quicker when clouds occasionally covered the sun. I camped by a nameless creek that added two thirds more volume to the river. The open country has given me more confidence in bear country, but I still worry and pray for safety and health. The weather continues to be outstanding, yet these rivers need some rain or I will have a whole lot more of what I had today. I am nearly finished reading *Shardik*. There is a tension here. I want to complete the story but this is bittersweet. The book has been a good companion. I have looked forward to reading it at the end of these long days.

I noticed the first yellow in the willows today. Arctic summers are short. There are clouds in the west tonight. I must keep a good attitude—be careful. I observe *Baetis* mayflies (blue-winged olives) dance in the air by the water in the cool evening light. This lightens my mood.

There was a ground fog the next morning. The fog moved out on the developing northwest breeze. The breeze intensified into a strong wind, and I laboriously struggled against it all day. The river remained difficult, alternating between shallow, floatable sections and rock riffles that forced me out of my canoe. These conditions slowed my progress, but I had some fun rides maneuvering through fast rapids. I passed Itilyiargiok Creek today. It drains a large basin, yet the water it adds to the Nigu is meager. Grayling swim in the crystal-clear river.

Late in the evening, before stopping to camp, I became confused about my location. There were no good landmarks to do an accurate triangulation. The 20-mile-per-hour wind chilled my enthusiasm. I finally camp on a gravel bar nearby with my position unresolved and I am cold now. Clouds push up against the mountains to the north, but it was relatively clear overhead. A feeling of vague uneasiness is over me this night—a battle that shifted between excessive fear and overconfidence. I must stay focused, be humble, yet stay confident in my abilities. I must be alert, aware, and not lose my temper. Seeing wildlife eases my mind. It gives life to an empty land. I enjoy the presence of long-tailed jaegers, arctic terns, mew gulls, scoters, and mergansers but I see no caribou today.

I got cold last night and had to wear a shirt inside my sleeping bag. It was foggy again in the morning. I continue my efforts to pinpoint my position. The blackflies and mosquitoes are bothersome. An arctic ground squirrel is voicing its displeasure that I am there. But mayflies fly silently in the gentle breeze. Finding my position is critical today because I need to locate the outlet creek that indicates the vicinity of my next portage to Etivlik Lake. The fog hampers my efforts. The map does not seem to fit any land features, but from a high hill, I eventually match a big bend in the river to the map that is supposed to represent it. Backtracking on the map from the bend, I could see where I had camped last night. From this point on, I was able to follow the land quite easily with 1/63,360-scale maps (one mile to the inch) that were published just last year. Orientating myself to the landscape was uplifting. I proceeded while the fog vanished. A gentle breeze blew. The sun shone bright and the Nigu glimmered in the light. The Nigu is beginning to show signs of becoming a big river, its channel widening and becoming deeper.

I reached the Etivlik Lake outlet creek and it looked like I could track my canoe up it. This was tempting, but in the end, I decided to go downstream a few more bends to where the river swings closest to the lake.
It was about a one-mile portage over the tundra. Mats of caribou hair lined the shore at this point. This is another major caribou crossing. The hair had washed up after floating free from shedding animals. The hair of caribou is hollow, like all in the deer family. It provides buoyancy and insulation from the cold to the animals. The wind had strengthened by this time, racing up the river, making headway difficult on the water. It caused problems for me on land also. The first obstacle of the portage was a 120-foot-high bank. It was crisscrossed by numerous caribou trails so a path was easy to find, but the wind ripped at the canoe, jerking and pushing me in all

directions. The struggle was revealed in my weaving course up the hillside. Once on top, however, the wind was at my back and the portage went smoothly.

Heading across the tundra, I intersected the outlet creek. It was still wide and deep in many places, but quite shallow in others. Dragging my canoe up this creek would have caused unnecessary wear on my canoe. American golden plovers were nesting on the drier uplands. These birds undergo extensive migrations and overwinter in South America. The lake outlet was trashy. Fuel and food cans, tinfoil, and cardboard were strewn about. Bernd Gaedeke has a tent platform in the vicinity where he brings clients during hunting season (we are no longer in the National Park and sports hunting is allowed) but this does not look like his kind of operation.

The area is a major archeological site. Mike Kunz, who I met in Bettles at the start of my trip, and many others have done intensive studies of semisubterranean house sites along Etivlik Lake (Kunz, 2005). The depressions of these houses were arranged in tiers in what looked like a major village. This would have been a winter village. These shelters were built to withstand the howling arctic winds. The area was also used in the nonwinter months but the people used caribou skin tents held down with rocks for shelters. Caribou was their main food but fishing was also important. Studies have shown that the earliest occupation of the area was about 3,500 years ago. These people were part of what is known as the Denbigh Flint Culture which is considered part of the Arctic Small Tool Tradition. Other traditions followed such as the Norton, Ipiutak, and late prehistoric Eskimo people but there is no evidence of the present Inupiat inhabiting the site. Etivlik Lake is at the hub of important travel corridors radiating out from the lake—Flora Creek to the Noatak River and Kotzebue Sound, the Nigu and Etivlik Rivers to the Colville River and the Beauford Sea, and the Alatna River which provides access to interior Alaska. Along with habitation, the area may have also functioned as a meeting place and trade center. The natural corridors I saw on the maps as I planned this trip and am now retracing were in fact used by the Denbigh Flint Culture people and others that followed as major routes in a vast travel and trading network.

I camped at the outlet among the broken bones of animals killed in the past, the strange remnants of a once-thriving village, and the modern trash of more recent visitors. Grayling swim in the creek and I managed to catch a few. A common loon called, sending ripples of sound through the calm evening.

It was July 31. I had been out on the land for thirty-two days. This was the longest wilderness trip of my life. I think of troubles I had with a past supervisor in Kotzebue. I will have to face this person at the end of the trip. Mind games. I want this trip to be successful but fleeting thoughts emerge that all is going too well and this is not very exciting. What if something should go wrong? No. I cannot think like this. I must concentrate on the positive—focus on being safe but also keep the trip enjoyable.

I have enjoyed this place. Breakfast includes manna (a mix of grains cooked as a hot cereal), Tang, and coffee. A walk reveals blooming Jacob's ladder and monkshood. The dwarf fireweed, saxifrage, and coltsfoot are already in seed. Summer flower season has long passed its peak. Three long-tailed jaegers are doing battle overhead.

I continued across Etivlik Lake. A strong quartering wind is now at my back and my canoe seems to have a mind of its own. It will not track in the direction I am trying to steer it. Instead, the canoe heads off in a 45-degree angle from my intended path. I must exert excessive power to put it right, or stop the forward motion of the canoe and start over. The canoe's behavior is a mystery.

CHAPTER 5

The Trials of Flora Creek

I paddled to the inlet stream and make a half-mile portage over low tussocks to a small lake. The portage at the end of this lake leads me over a nearly flat divide. This journey has now taken me into three distinct river basins. The first was the Alatna and Koyukuk Rivers that are part of the Yukon River Basin. The second was the Nigu River which flows down the arctic slope and is part of the Colville River Basin. And the third I have just entered—the headwaters of Flora Creek that leads to the Aniuk River which is part of the Noatak River Basin. I have also entered Noatak National Preserve, a 6,569,904-acre park area created by ANILCA in 1980, and left the National Petroleum Preserve Alaska (NPRA). I was in NPRA only briefly, crossing the farthest  south-central extension of the preserve. Administered by the Bureau of Land Management (BLM), NPRA is the largest tract of undisturbed public land in the United States (23,599,999 acres). I saw much evidence of caribou kills and a massive caribou migration. The kills

were probably made by wolves. All that is left of the prey animals are some hair, hide, and a few bones.

Ahead are the Inyorurak Lakes, the source of Flora Creek. The first of these is an expansive sheet of deep blue water about a mile and a half long. I look across its shimmering surface from a ridge above the lake. On the ridge, rock piles stretch out in a long row on both sides of a cut that leads down to the lake. These are the remnants of Inukshuks, an Inuit word meaning the semblance of man. Arctic hunters built these structures to fool caribou into thinking there was a line of people. Woman and children might stand in-between the structures waving their arms to enhance the illusion. Caribou heading in the general direction of the lake would try to avoid the perceived humans and be led into the confined area of the cut. Hidden hunters would be in wait to leap out and find the concentrated caribou easier to kill.

It is a warm day and the sun feels good. I could sense the presence of the ancient arctic people. It was a vague, uneasy feeling. Perhaps I was not having particularly reverent thoughts. I looked over the edge of the steep bank to the lakeshore. It seemed easiest to lead the canoe over the edge with the painter line instead of negotiating the bank while carrying it over my head. This I tried but something strange began to happen. As I led the canoe down slowly, it started angling to the left instead of dropping straight down. I fought this tendency at first but then let it go where it wanted. Nothing seemed to be directing its course from underneath. The canoe passed over brush along the bank but I was able to reach the shoreline without difficultly. Then I felt a sharp, burning pain into my left arm. I look down just in time to see a bee leaving after it had implanted its stinger in my flesh. I look up to the brush that I had just trampled through. Angry bees were swarming around the entrance of an underground nest. The canoe had led me over this nest. I was far enough away that no other bees were following me, but immediately I think, "What if I go into anaphylactic shock?" I have never had an allergic reaction to bee stings before but what if this is the first time? There would be no help. I needed to be calm. I get away from the bees, grab my lunch, and head up to the ridge to sit in the sun and relax. Yet I couldn't help feeling that I had received a message here. What it exactly was or why I received it I could not be sure. I believed it had something to do with respecting the land and those who had lived on it long ago and were so much a part of it.

My arm throbbed around the sting but it was not swelling appreciably. I was relieved at this because it meant that there was no severe reaction to the bee venom. After lunch, I explored around the area and identify wheatears,  American pipits, and Savannah sparrows. American golden-plovers were along the portage. Long-tailed jaegers feign defensive dives in my direction. A golden eagle glides over the lake. Two common loons paddle on the calm surface and talk to each other, not sure if my intrusion represented a threat. Their calls echo in the stillness of the afternoon. The breeding season was still underway and this country is

alive. It was an eerie feeling—the land seemed so close, so compressed, as if I was in the confinement of a room.

On the water, I paddled toward the outlet of this beautiful lake. It was calm and my canoe sliced through water easily and efficiently. Would there be enough water to float my canoe or was there going to be a long series of agonizing portages ahead? The outlet was initially wide and deep. Its waters flowed clear and slowly. Grass and algae covered the bottom and grayling up to 18 inches scurried for the cover of the deeper pools. I flushed a female common goldeneye with four ducklings and an American wigeon. I worked my way to Kikitaliorak Lake. This named lake is nearly the same size as the first lake. The wind had steadily increased and was blowing hard now from the west. I looked for shelter from the constant blow but the tundra yielded little. An island just offshore held promise, yet after bucking the wind and waves to get there, it provides no relief from the tyrannical gale. It held other interests, however. On its surface were several rock tent rings, food caches (cache pits), and other human structures. This was a possible summer site for an arctic people—those that came before the Inupiat. Also, there was a family of nesting glaucous gulls on the island. They were not happy that I was there. Five adults protested my presence as two chicks floated in a protective cove along the shore.

I returned to the inlet and found a campsite partially protected from the wind. The stream was alive with lake trout. I go a-fishin. They are hungry fish and ferociously attack any lure I present to them. The commotion of their brethren being caught makes no difference in their willingness to strike. I catch three and keep one about five pounds. The fish has nothing in its stomach which perhaps explains why they are in the creek. Food would be more plentiful there. I boil the fish to reduce the problem of lingering odors. Though a bit tougher cooked this way, the fish provides a nice change from the processed foods I have been eating. After dinner, I walk and am bathed in the golden arctic light.

I feel good that I have made it this far. It is August 1. Fog shrouds the land again this morning. As it starts to thin and clear, the sun produces a rainbow. Loons treated me to a full-throated chorus last night and during the dawn. They were in this lake but flew back toward the first lake while I was having a breakfast of pancakes and coffee. The lake is a mirror. My canoe glides through the still water, producing a slow spreading transformation of the surface. Snow-white glaucous gulls circle against a deep-blue sky. Their prattling is intended to keep me away from the same two downy chicks I saw yesterday, which are swimming calmly on the lake. I give them a wide berth and proceed on to the outlet.

The outlet is choked with sedges. I push through the thick vegetation and the long struggle with Flora Creek begins. Soon I reach a place that is blocked by a dense thicket of willows. Portaging was the only way around. Nightmarish memories flash through my mind. Is this going to be another Henshaw Creek? But the stream quickly opens up again and this is the end of willow bashing for the remainder of the trip. Passage down the creek continued to be difficult, however, because of its shallowness, but I still made good progress.

The upper creek meandered a great deal and was broken up by many small lakes. The bottom began as mud and gravel but

soon turned to rocks. Long stretches of shallow water and algae-covered rocks made walking a torture and caused excessive wear on the bottom of my canoe. The new fiberglass that Bernd Gaedeke provided had already worn through to the Kevlar along the keel line. I was hoping the worst is over and the creek would increase in volume farther downstream. I passed a large tributary coming in from the south that adds a small amount of water to the creek. I continued on until I reached a northern tributary flowing out of Inyorurak Pass where I stopped to camp. The creek was in a broad valley with low hills and mountains to the north and south. Large grayling and round whitefish were numerous in the productive stream. I saw a grizzly bear today, the third on this trip, but it was at least three miles away and walking rapidly to the west. Heat waves produced from the intense sun beating on the land distorted its image and gave it a ghost-like appearance.

Great thunderstorms swept across the arctic plains to the east. Sunlight and massive gray clouds contrasted in the big sky over the wide open yellow-green tundra. But I never felt a drop of rain. Marsh hawks patrolled the muskeg, greater scaup were rearing a family in a

small lake, American golden plovers were nesting in the uplands. Parasitic jaegers were hunting on the wing. Bird life kept the country alive with movement.

There is ice on my glove and steam drifts from the

surface of the creek and surrounding ponds this morning. The day is cloudless. It warms up as the sun moves higher in the sky. Mosquitoes and blackflies become active as the temperature rises. Oh, what a view of the open valley and distant mountains.

Last night, I dreamt of several friends, in particular, Steve and Carol Moss and Liz Bellantoni, all three of whom I worked with at Isle Royale National Park in 1980 and 1981. I also dreamt of walking down a river. No surprise there. I awake in good spirits and am anxious to see friends again.

Good spirits turn to bad as I become aware of what the river has in store for me today. Misery, misery, misery. Rocks stretch for miles. They are covered with algae and are dangerously slippery. I hit the ground hard in numerous falls. One quarter-mile section was covered with large, dry rocks. My canoe was completely out

of water as I dragged it down the riverbed. The wear on my canoe is frightening. Two and three layers of Kevlar are worn through in several places. Often, I thought the creek might completely disappear, especially after passing a major tributary that was totally dry.

A plane burst out of the west, flying low up the valley and roaring past me. It was Bernd Gaedeke making good on his word that he would check on me. The plane circled and flew by again, this time so low I could see Bernd's face clearly. He flashed a constrained smile as if to say there is trouble ahead, tipped his wings, and continued off to the east. The departure of the plane left a void of silence. I was elated to realize someone was out there who knew where I was. But I also felt alone, knowing that I was not likely to see anyone for a long time.

A grizzly bear appeared in the distance around midmorning. I came unexpectedly close to a second bear some time later. It was in an aggressive mode and may have just attacked and injured a caribou which I saw soon after with an injured leg. This sighting jolted me back to attention. I was in the arctic. Life and death struggles are going on before me and if I do not remain attentive, I could blunder into a bad situation. The bear never indicated it knew I was there but was moving away from the creek and could have easily heard or smelled me. I am sure I was detectable a long way off after not having had a bath for over a week. There was another bear in the distance later that day, the sixth grizzly sighting on the journey. But the strangest encounter I have ever experienced with a bear was yet to come. It was my custom to take a nap after eating lunch. The sun was warm this afternoon and I laid down on the gravel beside a small creek and quickly fell asleep. I was jarred awake by a commotion in the willows. Out stepped a grizzly about 50 feet from me on the opposite shoreline. As I stood up and grabbed my shotgun from the canoe, the bear took a few steps toward me. I yelled aggressively "Get out of here, bear," while fumbling to wrack a shell into the chamber of my shotgun. The bear backed off and continued upstream, eventually moving out of sight.

I calmed down a little and attempted to nap again, this time with my shotgun closer by my side. I was jolted awake again and bolted up with shotgun in hand staring at another commotion coming

from the exact location where the bear emerged. No bear appeared. But as I watched, a dust devil roared out of the willows, swept across the creek, and engulfed a willow bush slightly behind me and about eight feet away. It shook and rattled that bush with a thunderous noise and as I turned to look, I saw the bear I had seen earlier running up the hill behind me saturated in rich sunlight that was streaming through a break in the clouds. The scene was breathtaking and suddenly frightening. Another message? Could this bear have left part of itself behind which was making its presence known? I went back to my nap, but the images of the moment left me in awe and perhaps a bit confused. There was much more to this land than I could perceive.

The day was exhausting. I camped on tussock tundra high enough to have a good view. I had difficulty putting up my tent and preparing dinner. A large bull moose stood staring at me a short distance from camp. It decided I was not much of a threat and went back to eating willow leaves. Moose can survive the arctic winters as long as there are some large willows for cover and for food. They are expanding into the arctic along major river drainages. It was a good day for wildlife having seen this rare moose and four grizzly bears in the valley. The sun went down and it quickly turned chilly.

Stiffness makes it hard to move this morning. I finished *Shardik* last night and feel something akin to losing a close friend. I looked forward to reading this book for so many nights. I was emotionally involved with the characters and the big brown bear at the heart of the story. It doesn't seem like another book could take its place right now, but I will begin *Moby Dick* tonight, my third attempt to read it.

The wind is a frigid 20 miles per hour from the northwest. Paddling against it is wearisome, but I have little opportunity to do this. The boulder gardens disappeared, replaced with smaller rocks. The way remained torturous. Slippery rock surfaces sent me to the hard riverbed. Shallow water now exposes the bottom of the canoe to constant fraying and gouging from the substrate. The river is becoming more lowland in character. Large gravel bars are more common, there is less gradient, and some sand and mud bars are appearing. The water volume is steadily decreasing. At one point, the channel was only three feet across. The river becomes braided, spreading the low water even thinner. And finally, it happened. The creek simply disappeared. It went completely dry! I was standing on the parched river bed in an exhausted daze. My frustration exploded into a furious rage. I stomped around yelling at the top of my lungs. I eventually succumbed to self-pity, dropped to my knees, and wept.

After venting these emotions, I sat up and ate lunch in a disheartened gloom. With food in my stomach, my attitude improved  and I was finally resolved to my situation. I pulled myself up and took a walk down the dry creek bed. To my great joy I found water emerging from the gravel and the river began flowing again a quarter of a mile downstream. I think of the saying "The darkest hour is right before the dawn." After I made the short portage, the water was deep enough and I was able to paddle all the way to the junction with the Aniuk River.

I brimmed with joy as I watched that river blending its waters with Flora Creek. I thought my low water problems were over. This was the farthest north the trip would take me—68 degrees 9 minutes north latitude. Only a little over a mile to the northeast lies a low corridor through the Brooks Range called Howard Pass. It was late in the evening and the sun poured onto the tundra, which emanated saturated colors of green and yellow. Long shadows accented river cuts. It was a wonderful time to be alive. I turned the corner and began paddling southwest with plenty of water and a strong current underneath me. The wind was at my back. Parasitic and long-tailed jaegers kept me company. I flushed a short-eared owl along Flora Creek earlier and marsh hawks commonly patrolled the living tundra.

I saw many other birds today along the river and creek: glaucous gulls, arctic terns, red-necked phalaropes, lesser yellowlegs, semipalmated plovers, American golden plovers, American pipits, arctic warblers, American wigeons, red-breasted mergansers, and a surf scoter.

I continued on to Fauna Creek and camped at the confluence. This compliment of Flora Creek was low but still issued a large volume of water into the Aniuk River. Any increases in water volume were appreciated. The strong wind blowing out of Howard Pass was cold. I huddled in my campsite to stay warm at the base of the Pupik Hills.

The wind was still blowing the next morning and a ground fog blotted out the sun. It was August 4. I moved back into the tent after breakfast to stay warm while writing in my journal. The riverbed was strewn with boulders and I struggled again with low water. There were long stretches of rocks and riffles to work through. Deeper paddling water was rare at first but increased as the day progressed.

The day became hot and sunny. It reached into the 80s when the wind was still. The colorful rocks shone through the crystal-clear river.

I ate lunch at the confluence of Rough Mountain Creek. This extensive drainage heads just south of the Flora Creek headwater lakes and winds around the tundra for miles before joining the Aniuk. It adds a good volume to the river. All the other major tributaries were dry. I saw a Pacific loon in the river earlier. Thunderstorms towered in the east during the late afternoon and I felt the first drops of rain in weeks. The last squall ended in a rainbow that built slowly, but eventually developed a full arch across the sky as the sun was setting. I had lost track of time and was on the river unusually late.

Soon after seeing the rainbow, I was lining my canoe through a riffle area adjacent to a steep bluff. I was observing nesting rough-legged hawks and whitewater noise dominated my senses. But through this, I thought I heard a bark. I turned to look and standing only 25 feet behind me was a wolf. It was light-colored and appeared thin yet determined. It continued to bark aggressively at me but eventually crossed the river and moved upstream. Between the barks were half howls. Finally, it left the shoreline and climbed onto the tundra. I was dazed and did not think to grab my camera until then. I ran and scrambled up the bank, but the wolf had moved well away from me. Her barking persisted. I guessed she had pups in the area, and this was a rendezvous site where adults were watching over and training the pups before being fully initiated into the pack. This suspicion was strengthened when, farther downriver, I heard a strange yippy bark that sounded like an eerie laugh. It was another wolf on the tundra adamant that I should leave. This animal was larger, darker, and seemed in better condition though it was bothered by insects. I assumed it was a male because of its size. I left the wolves in peace and continued downriver to look for a campsite. I never felt threatened by these wolves. Even though their behavior was somewhat mysterious, it would be consistent with good parenting and protecting their young.

While moving past steeper bluffs, two adult rough-legged hawks swooped down to scold me. I could see two fledglings near the nest. A little way past this, I found a nice gravel bar for camping next to a deep pool. There was a 60-foot bluff on the other side of the river. Beyond were the rounded Pupik Hills. There are many dead fish on the river bottom. I could see no obvious cause for the fish kill. I was able to identify at least one round whitefish.

Sleeping was difficult the next morning because I was excited about reaching the Noatak River today. It was August 5. There was much willow driftwood around and I built a small fire. Time to burn trash and clean up a food bag where honey leaked. Ravens are hanging around my camp. I had a late breakfast of pancakes, coffee, and a bacon bar. It is warm and dry—no dew formed last night. There is something odd about the day, something different in the hazy air. I finally realize it is the smell of burning leaves. Somewhere to the south, a

wildland fire is burning. It smells like a tundra fire which may have been started from yesterday's thunderstorms. The land is incredibly dry right now.

The river remains shallow and rocky, interspersed more frequently with deeper, slow water sections.

Despite the thunderstorms, the river was still dropping and gin clear. Not long after getting underway, two wolf pups gallop across the river. One disappeared as soon as it saw me, the other hung on to a bone they were fighting over, ran about 50 feet, plopped down, and began gnawing on its prize. I jumped out of the canoe to approach the pup, but it gets to its feet and moves a little farther away and sits down again. We play this game for a while, me approaching the pup and it moving just out of camera range, until the pup finally slips out of sight into the brush. I would guess the pups were about 10 to 12 weeks old. Ravens watched the game, waiting perhaps for a scrap of food left by the commotion. These pups were in the same vicinity as the adults I observed yesterday and I am quite sure they are all part of one extended family.

Later in the day, I was deep in thought and not attentive to my surroundings when I caught a glimpse of a moving brown form on the left bank. It was gone before I could determine what it was. Was it a bear or wolf? My curiosity needed to be satisfied so I climbed onto the tundra and peered down river. A grizzly bear, now 150 feet away, was standing upright on two legs, with nose high, testing the air and looking back in my direction. It dropped back down on all fours and made its way to the river. I returned to the canoe. Next, I could see the bear was walking toward me. I grabbed my shotgun, racked a shell in the chamber, and yelled, "Hey, Bear!". The bear bolted into the willows on the opposite shore. I cautiously move by the place where the bear was last seen but it did not reappear. This was the eighth grizzly bear seen on this trip.

Birdlife was varied, especially as I approached the Aniuk River mouth. A golden eagle flew overhead. Birds on the water included surf scoters, red-breasted mergansers, and a Pacific loon. I moved past a large, nameless tributary on my right that added some volume to the river. Paddling was good now; my heart quickened. Several bends remained, but at last, I turned a corner and there before me was a water super highway through the wilderness—the Noatak River. I waved my paddle high into the air and yelled with unmitigated joy. Water, deep-flowing water! My canoe dragging days were over for this trip. Well, not quite. The Aniuk forced me to pull the canoe over one last shallow section before I could enter the waters of the Noatak.

CHAPTER 6

The Noatak

The earliest recorded exploration of the Noatak River by nonnatives was in 1885 by S. B. McLenegan of the Revenue Steamer *Corwim*. He traveled with a seaman named Nelson. They moved upstream to the headwaters in a 27-foot skin boat. It seems a strange coincidence that I am exploring the river for the first time exactly one hundred years later.

The current grabbed my canoe as I dug deep with the paddle, and it flew effortlessly downriver. The blue tinted water was slightly murky. A cross fox trotted along the shoreline. I paddled another long bend before stopping to camp, thinking the most difficult and dangerous part of my journey was behind me. But I knew that now was no time to let down my guard. Nothing had changed. I must

think safety and stay alert. My fatigue was complete this day. Mosquitoes were troublesome in the evening until the sun started to set and the air cooled rapidly. The Aniuk River had taken me out of the mountains into the Aniuk lowlands. This nearly featureless landscape has been obscured all day by the persistent haze.

I head to the Cutler Ranger Station today. There is still a smoky haze in the air, but the sun penetrates the haze and sheds its warmth on the land. The morning is quiet. A Pacific loon floats by on the swift current. The river is fun to float with a few Class II rapids to negotiate and I only hit bottom twice. The country has little relief and wildlife is scarce. It has an oppressive, empty feeling. Clouds rolled in by midafternoon then rain falls briefly. Winds build to 30 miles per hour on the heels of the squall but diminish later in the afternoon.

Shortly after getting started this morning, I came across the first people I had seen since staying at Bernd Gaedeke's place ten days ago. They were a rafting party of four clients. Their guide is Steve Giesler. I talked to Steve briefly and he said he had just come down the river with Karen Jettmar, who I had met while working for the NPS. They passed through here on July 13. Both Steve and Karen are associated with a guide service out of Anchorage.[7] The group was enjoying a leisurely trip down the river, getting suntans, drinking, and fishing while their guide struggled with the raft that is a large, broad target for the wind. Meeting this group was a big letdown. I was suddenly among tourists, a sharp contrast to the solitary remoteness and wilderness of the Nigu and Aniuk River valleys. The feeling of the trip had radically changed.

Around 3:00 p.m., I reached the Cutler Ranger Station which is located a few bends above the mouth of the Cutler River. The station consisted of two wall tents. The low water had exposed a quarter of a

---

[7] Karen Jettmar wrote a definitive guidebook on floating Alaska Rivers called *The Alaska River Guide: Canoeing Kayaking, and Rafting in the Last Frontier,* 3rd ed., Menasha Ridge Press, 2008.

mile of gravel bar that separated the station from the river. Nobody was around so I explored the area and read *Moby Dick*.

The ranger and her partner returned from an exploration trip to a mountain behind some bluffs on the south side of the river. Ranger Sam Eischeid was an attractive woman who was going to college in Montana. She had worked for Glacier National Park and knew another friend of mine—Greg Moss. Sam told me that many friends I worked with in 1983 were still working for the Northwest Area parks, including, Lee Ann Ayers, Harry Douglas, and Jon Petterson. She had been out all summer and had found it hard to adjust to the isolation and new a partner every few weeks. She was also missing trees. Alan Tickett was her Inupiat partner. He was a quiet man from Shungnak, a village along the Kobuk River.

We moved up to the ranger station to eat dinner and watched the colorful sunset that was the result of the smoky haze in the air. Sam and Alan treated me to a wonderful meal of broiled caribou, real potatoes, hot chocolate, and soup. The caribou was courtesy of Don Schmuckal. Don was a Kobuk Valley National Park ranger in 1983 stationed at the Onion Portage cabin the same year I worked for the park. Instead of a cabin, though, my Inupiat partner and I had to establish the Kallarichuk Ranger Station (a single wall tent) at the west end of the park. Don and I explored the Hunt River and the Kobuk Sand Dunes together. Sam mentioned that he was now doing FirePro work that involved mapping previous wildland fires and fire potential on the landscape using satellite and aerial photo images and collecting plants on the ground. Much of the work is done in remote areas accessible only by helicopter.

We did not finish cooking in time. A thunder and lightning storm slammed us and we got wet before getting into the tent. It was past midnight by the time we finished eating. We talked way beyond midnight. Sam said there had not been many groups floating by here this summer. This contributed to her feeling of isolation. Maybe the low water had kept them away. There was also not much to do or explore here and they had not seen much wildlife.

Sam went down to the river to wash up and found a very peculiar thing. I had moved my canoe some distance up the bank when I arrived and turned it upside down to secure it for the night. When Sam reached the river, she found it sitting upright with its bow resting on the gravel and its stern floating in the water. The canoe was sitting as if it was ready to move on. How was it transported to the river's edge? I went down and moved the canoe farther up the gravel bar then tied it to the ranger's motor boat.

We all wondered that night what forces were at work. Alan told a family story of when they had built a house where a shaman once lived. One corner of the room was haunted. If they forgot and let somebody sleep there, the visitors always woke up screaming from nightmares. One night, when he came into the house in the dark, he felt something like sand or pebbles shower him from the direction of that corner. He turned on the lights but nothing was there. Alan was convinced that spirits moved my canoe tonight.

The morning is damp and peaceful. It is August 7, my thirty-ninth day out. A ground fog cloaks the land but does not look like it will stay around long. There is the smell of fall in the air, especially around camp  where the willows have turned yellow.

We have char for breakfast, also compliments of Don Schmuckal and then we talk while the sun streams through the tent. It is 2:00 p.m. before I am back on the water heading for the Cutler River mouth. It had clouded up and begun to rain. I found the rafters' camp at the river mouth, but they were apparently upriver. Four Germans wave as they float by in two Old Town Tripper canoes. Their destination is Noatak Village. The Cutler is a pretty river—wide near the mouth with green terraces embracing its valley. It would be interesting to explore in the future. There is a route up the Cutler over a relatively low Bairds Mountains pass into the Redstone River. The Redstone joins the Amber River which is a tributary of the Kobuk River. The Ambler River enters the Kobuk near the village of Amber.

I paddled hard from the Cutler, covering over 20 miles. A massive thunder and lightning storm nearly blew me off the river on route. The canoe veered and pitched out of control from the gale force tailwind. Paddling on open water in this storm was not the safest place to be. I stopped to camp at the wide, expansive meander called Okak Bend. Several pairs of rough-legged hawks had taken advantage of the Bend's high river bluffs to build their nests in relative safety from predators. Another drenching rain followed. The rain stopped long enough for me to set up camp and eat dinner but started again as I finished cleaning up and crawled into the tent for the night.

A light rain was falling the next morning. A cool wind was blowing from the south. I continued down the Noatak. Vistas opened on the now hilly country. The overcast was gradually breaking up, but the wind remained strong and biting. I did not want to stop long for rests. Pacific loons cruised the river and rough-legged hawks kept watch on their bluffy outposts. I sailed pass Makpik Creek that flows out of Feniak Lake and also reached the mouth of Anisak River. I saw smoke from the river and walked inland to inspect the tundra fire. The billowing and dense white smoke was being pushed to the northwest. It smelled like wet, burning leaves. The country was so dry that the recent rain could not dampen the fire's spread. The tundra soaked up any available moisture.

Mew and glaucous gull fledglings were actively vocalizing on the wing. They usually traveled in threes. Life is present yet I no longer expect to see large wildlife[8] because sightings have been so rare. The country does not feel as wild and remote as I expected. It is an anti-climax after the intimate struggles with the land and surprise encounters with wildlife in the Upper Alatna, Nigu, and Flora Creek country. I find myself anxious to finish the trip. Meeting groups like the rafters and seeing more trash on the river bars contributes to this frame of mind.

The river has generally been pleasant to travel on, and I should be able to relax a little because I know that time is no longer pressing, yet I plod ahead in my inefficient canoe like paddling on a treadmill. My progress seems tediously slow, especially in the many slackwater areas where headwinds have hammered me. Pushing forward in these conditions grows tiresome. My butt hurts; my back aches. The paddle forms calluses on my hands just as they were beginning to

---

[8] Most of the caribou had traveled north of the Noatak River at the time of year I moved through the country. Grizzly bears are occasionally seen in the river corridor (saw one in 1991when floating the Noatak for the Western Arctic Parklands) but they seem to prefer the open tundra country of the upper Alatna, Nigu, and Flora Creek. Muskoxen (*Ovibos moschatus*) have been seen recently along the Noatak River corridor. They were extirpated from Alaska by the late 1800s.They were reintroduced in 1935 when 34 animals were captured from Greenland and brought to Nunivak Island where they thrived. In 1970 and 1977, 70 Nunivak animals were introduced at Cape Thompson. This population expanded its range south and east into Cape Krusenstern National Monument and Noatak National Preserve where the population numbers have remained stable. I saw twelve members from this group south of the Red Dog Mine Road when working in Cape Krusenstern NM in 1991.

heal from the damage inflicted by rope and water when dragging the canoe across miles of rocky river bottoms. Still, I covered over 37 miles today.

The weather has changed. Gone is the dry air and sunny skies that I enjoyed for weeks. I am now closer to hard elements—the biting wind and driving rain.

An unmarked rapids just before Itimtikrak Creek gives me a scare. Big waves menacingly materialized as I tried to negotiate the sharp bend walled in by steep bluffs. The whitewater pummeled my canoe and nearly filled it with water. That was a sobering ride. The river still holds surprises and I must respect its power. I cannot forget where I am. Danger is waiting if I do not stay focused. Yet I am not here to fear every moment. It is time to relax and enjoy this expedition I have worked so hard to plan and execute.

Good campsites were difficult to find as the late afternoon turned into evening. Rainbows appeared and intensified when the sun broke through the clouds. They arched across the sky, then diminished as rain took over again. After the rapids, the river channel was virtually straight for five miles. I camped on a stony river bar that was totally

exposed and this provided an excellent view up and down the river on this turbulent evening. The light shone bright again before sunset, but rain threatened before I retire. Despite the rain, the river appears to be getting clearer each day.

Rain intersperses with sunshine on this cool morning. It is August 9. The strong south wind penetrates me to my core. I start late knowing it's only about 12 miles to the Nimiuktuk River. That is my destination today.

Yet it seems to take a long time. Headwinds and still water impede my progress. I pass New Cottonwood Creek, named for the scrawny balsam poplar (*Populus balsamifera*) that grow along its banks, but do not see the cabin that the map shows is supposed to be in the area. The river is moving out of the Aniuk Lowlands and the rolling hills have replaced the broad, flat valley. The Kingasivik Mountains rise abruptly ahead, marking the course of the Nimiuktuk River. These mountains are part of the DeLong Mountains that span west and north of here and include major tributary headwaters of the Noatak River such as the Kugururok and Kelly Rivers. The DeLongs were named for the arctic explorer Lt. Commander George Washington De Long who died in the Lena River Delta, in November 1881, after his ship, the *Jeannette,* was crushed by sea ice while exploring off the coast of Serbia.[9]

I am going to take a rest day by Nimiuktuk River and fish for char. The Noatak flows strong and deep in places, making for a pleasant ride in some stretches. I regularly see large fish jumping. A gull was feeding on a spawned-out salmon at the mouth of a creek. Ravens travel in twos and threes, flying in intricate patterns. The ever-present gulls are defensive, perhaps because the young ones are ranging farther from the nest into more dangerous territory. I see several wheatears along the river. They have a long journey ahead of them. Alaskan wheatears winter on the savannas of northern and eastern Africa.

The rain is light and sporadic. The sun makes several appearances. I reach the Nimiuktuk in the early afternoon. After eating lunch, I set up camp and go fishing. Chum salmon are milling around in deep water near shore and some are in an advanced spawning condition. Females are digging redds. With a medium-sized spoon,

---

[9] An excellent account of the Jeannette's voyage is in the book *In the Kingdom of Ice* by Hampton Sides (2014).

I catch two large males with strongly hooked jaws embedded with sharp, protruding teeth. These powerful fish still have lots of energy. At another entrance channel of the Nimiuktuk River was a deep pool and I catch three salmon there, all around ten pounds. These fish looked like new arrivals searching for a way in to the Nimiuktuk. But the summer drought has left the river too low, even at its mouth, for fish to enter.

There is no fresh sign indicating the presence of large mammals but birds keep things interesting. I saw a group of five whimbrels yesterday. Pacific loons are using the river for breeding. A red-breasted merganser family lives near my campsite. I occasionally see a northern shrike chasing a sparrow.

This is a place that many people stop. Human footprints abound and there is a strange fire pit in the sand. Large logs cross the pit and act as support for smaller sticks and duff which cover the top. Perhaps it is used as a baking pit.

The decision to stay here was tough. I am counting the days to the end of the trip, but I do not want to rush out of the country when I can afford the time to see it. The charm of this place is immediately felt and I am happy to be able to relax and not have to worry about traveling tomorrow. I will explore the Nimiuktuk instead.

CHAPTER 7

The Nimiuktuk and Kelly Rivers

It is August 10 and I have been out for six weeks. It is hard to believe this much time has passed. How long will it be until I finish the trip? I am guessing ten days. The overcast sprinkles intermittent rain, but the sun is shining through a few layers of clouds. It is another peaceful morning.

I begin the walk up the Nimiuktuk. The Kingasivik Mountains dominate the view to the north. Rolling hills stretch to the south. Past the bluffs north of camp, the river runs through a flat gravel plain. It braids into  multiple, shallow channels with no real pools. Aufeis is left in patches from the winter, dripping in the 55-degree temperature and looking like stranded icebergs. It seems to attract a wide variety of bird life. Three kinds of gulls—mew, glaucous, and herring—are present and defensive because of their fledgling young. Ruddy turnstones in groups of three to six feed along the water's edge. Sandpipers flee from my approach.

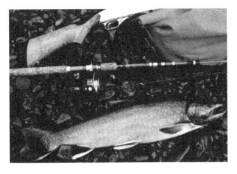

Beyond the gravel flats, the vegetation has taken hold. Willows, dwarf birch, and fireweed dominate the river bars. Big, juicy blueberries are abundant in the understory. Animal sign also increases. Grizzly bear, wolf, moose, and caribou tracks crisscross the sand, silt, and mud. And one massive pile of bear scat was heart-stopping. The river becomes more consolidated and deeper. Long pools began to appear. Farther upriver, I start to fish for char. They were not in the pools but on their spawning grounds in fast, waist-deep water. I hook a male in vivid spawning colors about 30 inches with a strongly hooked jaw. These sea-run char are aggressive and powerful. Generally called arctic char, or simply trout, by the Inupiat, they are actually a northern variety of Dolly Varden char (*Salvelinus malma malma*). The fish fights hard. It has the colors of an arctic sunset—red belly and dark back with orange spots, cream white edges of the pectoral, pelvic, and anal fins. The word *char* comes from a Gael word meaning "blood-red."

Northern Dolly Varden char have a complex life cycle. They are anadromous, meaning they feed as adults at sea (salt water) and come into their home freshwater streams to spawn. Mature fish spend the warmer months undergoing extensive migrations at sea. Some Alaska northern char, tagged to track their movements, have been caught in Russian waters, a journey of over 1,000 miles. Northern char enter freshwater rivers to overwinter. These rivers are usually not their spawning streams. They seek deepwater refuges influenced by springs or flowing groundwater until the next year's ocean migration or spawning run. The lower Noatak River from the mouth of the Kugururok River downstream to about 20 miles below Noatak Village is a char overwintering area.

I place this beautiful char in a cool, shady location and continue to fish. I catch and release a number of other char which seem to get smaller as I proceed up river. Spawning behavior is well underway. There is much redd digging and territorial squabbling. Chum salmon are also in the river but in lesser numbers. Many look like their life cycle is nearly complete. All five North American species of Pacific salmon in the genus *Oncorhynchus* die after spawning. Their bodies decompose in and around their spawning rivers to add nutrients which fuel the stream ecosystem and support the next generation of stream invertebrates and fish. These sea-run Dolly Varden char, on the other hand, often survive spawning to return to the sea, recover, and eventually make another spawning run.

I walk approximately five miles upstream close to a minor tributary that comes in from the west. This is a remarkable river and I wished I could continue walking on up the valley. Fall seems just around the corner here—the smells, color changes, and the wonderfully plentiful blueberries. I spend over an hour collecting blueberries (*Vaccinium uliginosum*), looking over my shoulder often to make sure that a bear is not doing the same thing in my immediate vicinity. I religiously carry the eight-pound shotgun. The decision to bring it as bear protection came with the commitment to have it with me at all times ready to use. It was never needed, though I was glad to have it on a few occasions. No bears sighted this afternoon but I did encounter a cow moose.

The mountains unfolded in sunshine briefly and then comes a hard rain. I get soaked and immediately feel chilled. It is time to head back to camp. I had left the first char I caught in willows beside the stream and have trouble finding it on the return trip. Cold and tired now, I am impatient and begin a frantic search. What a black note to a perfect day should I lose this fish and reach camp empty-handed. But at last, I find it laid out as it had been left and I was ecstatic. The cool, moist day preserved the rich colors of the fish. I carefully pick it up, feeling its eight-pound heft and resume my journey back to camp.

Shortly after finding the fish, I came upon a merlin family of five. *Chee, chee, chee,* cries ring out through the crisp air as both the young and adults protest my intrusion. Their flight is playful and acrobatic as they interweave around each other.

 I was going to build a fire this evening but the rain and late hour of my return encouraged me to boil the char instead. The pink-fleshed fish was tender and flavorful. To complement it, I have mashed potatoes and hot chocolate. And for dessert are fresh, juicy blueberries sprinkled with sugar. It is hard to describe such a meal after weeks of freeze-dried and processed foods. I am content and happy after this memorable day and feel refreshed to resume my trek down the Noatak tomorrow.

The sun is shining this morning. There are whitecaps on the blue water. A strong westerly wind is blowing and lenticular clouds stroke the sky. It is a cold morning. The river has risen about five inches yet remains clear. I have blueberry pancakes for breakfast and feel their energy will brace me for this fallish day. At the western channel, where the Nimiuktuk enters the Noatak, is a cabin owned by Abraham Howarth. I visit it before heading down river. He had an open invitation to stay there for anybody traveling on the river. I might have taken him up on it had I known it was there earlier. His only request was to leave the place clean. It was a simple but comfortable cabin. The entries in the cabin logbook were interesting. One person was rudely surprised when a grizzly bear knocked open the door. Apparently, the bear was also surprised at finding a human in the cabin and went on about its business. There was a log entry from Jon Peterson, a ranger I had worked with in 1983, and Jim Minnerath, who I did not know, but when I went to Utah State University, I had a photographer friend named Mike Minnerath. Could they be related? They were both from Kansas. I found out later that they are brothers. It is a small world.

The paddling day gets off to a bad start. The wind is gusting to 30 miles per hour, and I have to face it head-on in a wide, slow section of the river. Waves have built to three feet. Inching along, I work my way west for about  two miles where the river turns southwest. It is better after this but remains cold. Annoying, intermittent rain showers blow in on squalls, but they are short, and the sun pokes through the clouds, adding its blessed warmth and endless variation of light patterns to the land. Several rainbows appear and fade. Rough-legged hawks guarded most of the riverside bluffs. In the afternoon, I saw an animal from a distance that looked like a wolverine. When I pulled up to the spot where I last saw the animal, I could find no tracks. This was strange because the soil was soft mud and had many other older tracks embedded in it. I wondered if the animal could have been a cross fox but it had a slinky gate like a wolverine. Years later I was told by a research biologist that wolverines are incredibly light on their feet and often do not leave tracks.  A little way downriver, I see a bird perched on a shoreline rock that looks like a falcon. Studying it from a distance, I detect a black hood around the eye and a gray back, revealing it to be a peregrine falcon, but I do not get very close to it before it flies off.

There were more sections with good current after lunch and I made decent time despite the strong wind. The country is closing in with mountains and rolling hills approaching nearer to the river. I was entering the broad area known as the Grand Canyon of the Noatak, though there is no canyon or spectacular scenery that this name would imply. It is pleasant country to travel through, however, and a big change from the Aniuk Lowlands. I can see 20 feet to the river bottom. Its clarity, blueness, and rocky depths remind me of Lake Superior. I camp on a rough gravel bar somewhat protected from the wind by willows. I enjoy a fine view up the river. The rich smell of fall is in the air. I paddled about 23 miles today.

The morning is still on this August 12. I have been out 44 days. I heard strange sounds last night and got up twice to check on rocks being moved on the shoreline and birds sounding alarm calls around camp. I never figured out what it was.

The river drifts by silently. Robins are common now in the willows. The cool dampness is accentuated by occasional rain drops. I get a good start and paddle efficiently. The clouds increase through the morning. An old Fish and Wildlife Service cabin sits an inconvenient quarter mile from the river and I stop to take a look. The Kelly River Rangers have been up here only once this season. Wildlife is scarce. I see one lone caribou.

The wind grows stronger and the clouds thicken. The rain starts—light in the beginning, but turning into a steady, long duration drizzle by late afternoon. I come around a bend and pass Kuyak Creek. Tall spires shatter the outline of the open sky. These are white spruce trees on the horizon, the first I had seen since the Alatna River. Straight and tall, their smell wafts on the wind and memories of the forest return. This is the first of many patches of spruce trees I will encounter during the rest of the trip. I have crossed an arctic treeline, a testament of the regional climatic effects of the large river.

My anticipation is high. Whitewater had not been much of a problem on the Noatak, but there was potential trouble ahead. It was the Noatak Canyon.  Steep, sheer cliffs (Sekuiak Bluff) force the powerful river into a narrow channel. No major rapids are there, but I had been warned about some high waves. It was cool and misty as I approach. To prepare for whitewater, I take off my Servus Neoprene boots so that I can get my feet underneath my seat and kneel in the bottom of the canoe. It is too close to the end of my trip to take any unnecessary chances. The veiling rain enveloped the mountains and the Canyon, evoking a somber and mysterious mood. In dark silence, the waves well up at the canyon mouth. I brace and steady the canoe, taking in the bumpy ride. And that quickly it is over. The swift current is smooth after that and it propels me by the massive rock walls. I stay on my guard but the river remains gentle.

I paddled late and nearly reached the mouth of the Kugururok River where I camped on a high, sandy bar with willows behind. The site has an open view of the river but rain obscures it. I am cold and wet but the cagoule (a waterproof, knee-length type of anorak) I am wearing helps keep my upper body dry. It was getting dark. I eat a quick freeze-dried meal and dive for the warmth and dryness of the tent.

It is windy, cold, and rainy in the morning—so miserable that I stay in bed and read. As the rain pounds the tent, I wonder if it is worth proceeding the short distance to the Kelly River where I will take another rest day. I eventually get up, relieve myself, and cook a breakfast of pancakes. There is overcast close to the ground and I would face a strong headwind. The river is up two inches.

I am dirty, my pants are mildewing, and my socks are rotting. Will the Kelly ranger even let me in? I finally pack up and get under way. My watch has stopped and I have no idea what time it is. The sun is already in the west. The clouds begin to break up. The rain quits. The wind has lessened too. I proceed towards the Kelly in the gray light, enjoying the country but finding it confusing. I was apparently shuttled off into channels that are not on the map. The country opens up and the mountains are clearly visible. In the late evening, sunshine bathes the nearby hills intermittently. I noticed greater chum salmon activity.

No one is there when I arrive at the ranger station. I eat the last of the Nimiuktuk char and wait. Dana Hoyle and her Inupiat partner Mike finally return from cleaning up trash left on the Kelly River Bar by a party group from Kotzebue. We talk awhile in the dark. Dana had worked at Malone Bay in Isle Royale National Park a couple of seasons and was originally from Flint, Michigan. I had worked for Isle Royale in 1980 and 1981, a few summers before her. I express my surprise to see the changes at this station. The Park has built two wooden tent frames—one for cooking and one for sleeping. This was a big improvement to the single wall tent that I was issued in 1983 when I was a backcountry ranger on the Kobuk River. I set up my tent outside instead of using their shelter and it was dark before we went to bed.

It is a glorious sunny morning—warm and not a breath of wind. I was camped by the river and heard salmon jumping all night. Gulls were arguing over spawned-out salmon scraps in the early morning hours. Mike was due to leave for the Cutler Ranger Station. These Inupiat Resource Technicians worked at a ranger station two weeks at a time. They were rotated from station to station throughout the summer, giving them a wide variety of experience.

Lee Anne Ayers and Ray Bane, both friends from past seasons working for the Park Service, flew in today. Ray Bane is a pilot and anthropologist. He has done early subsistence research that provided baseline data for establishing management policy in Alaska arctic parklands. I knew him from Gates of the Arctic when I worked there in 1982. He told great stories about traveling in the arctic by dogsled. He had said many times that winter was the truth about Alaska. Lee Anne was a research biologist for the Northwest Areas (Three areas administered by one Superintendent: Kobuk Valley National Park, Noatak National Preserve, and Cape Krusenstern National Monument) when I met her in 1983 before heading to my station on the Kobuk River.[10] It was warm reunion. We talked about old times, ate, and updated each other on our lives. Lee Anne stayed to do some vegetation work around camp. She was working on determining the diet of Dall sheep (*Ovis dalli dalli*). They eat willows, she told me, but not the mat willows. They feed primarily on feltleaf willows (*Salix alaxensis*). They also eat the flower heads lousewort (*Pedicularis*) and *Oxytropis nigrescens*. There is not much

---

[10] This area is now administered by the NPS as the Western Arctic National Parklands and includes Kobuk Valley National Park, Noatak National Preserve, Cape Krusenstern National Monument, and Bering Land Bridge National Preserve.

Dryas, sedge, or grasses available in the higher elevations where they live. She told me she is pursuing her airplane pilot's license.[11] Ray headed back to Kotzebue.

Dana and I went fishing on the Kelly River. We each caught a female char full of eggs. One fish had a few salmon eggs in its stomach and the other had fish entrails in its gut. This area gets heavy fishing pressure and as groups clean their fish, they toss the entrails into the river, making them available for char. Sea-run char are thought to stop feeding once they enter fresh water, but stomach contents of these fish seem to indicate some scavenging by char does take place. There was a report of a grizzly bear up the Kelly but we didn't see it. Lee Anne looked around old Enik Sherman's cabin. The Inupiat man is old and blind but he would still rather be here than in the village of Noatak. Back at camp, our fish made a delectable meal served with Rice-A-Roni and wine. It was a good day with old and new friends.

It began to rain in the late afternoon. It continued all night and all the next day. I held up at the Kelly another day. Dana and Lee Anne stayed put also. There was no need to travel in this miserable weather. The mountains were obscured by the low ceiling. The day was spent reading and eating. A group of five people from Tennessee in three Old Town Tripper canoes stopped by the station. They put in at Pingo Lake in Gate of the Arctic National Park and had been on the river for eleven days. We have a friendly interchange and talk a long time about the country, my trip, park legislation, and other weighty subjects. Their views reflect "lower 48" attitudes about subsistence. They did not understand why natives (rural residents) should be allowed to use motorboats, snow machines, and high-powered rifles for subsistence activities in a Wilderness National Park area. They head off to make camp on the Kelly Bar.

---

[11] Lee Anne Ayres eventually got her pilot's license and was hired as a Wildlife Biologist/Pilot for Selawik National Wildlife Refuge.

Dana prepared spaghetti with a clam sauce and we finished the rest of the char. To top it off we had pistachio pudding. I was full but had no worries about overeating. There is little fat on me now. I have lost over fifteen pounds on this trip. It is 100 miles to the mouth of the Noatak and I anticipate this will take at least three days to complete. I am ready to move on.

CHAPTER 8

The Final Days on the Noatak

The sky is blue with only a few lenticular clouds on this August 16 morning. The cool wind out of the northeast should be at my back. I say goodbye to Dana and Lee Anne. We take pictures and I push off into the speedy current. I pass a group led by Bettles guide Dave Ketcher. He is guiding six people plus his son, Jason. They had camped at the Kelly River Bar the night before. His son mentioned picking up part of a mastodon tusk on the trip and had found mastodon molars up a side canyon. It is illegal to take these paleontological artifacts from any federal land. The group eventually catches up to me and we travel together at different times throughout the day and cross paths many other times. The tailwind builds to 15 miles an hour and the river is swift. We are making incredible time.

The Noatak River Valley has broadened into a vast plain, dotted with tundra ponds and the mountains are far in the distance shrouded in a blue haze. The Noatak splits into numerous braids but all run fast and deep. I have to make sure not to get shunted off in a braid that would obscure Noatak Village, so I stay close to the right side of the river. I want to stop and get some candy bars. There are virtually no landmarks to key in on which means I am never quite sure of my position. We are outside the National Preserve now. Many subsistence camps are along the river and late in the day, two motorboats pass me. The villagers would normally go farther upstream over the summer but water levels were too low this year.

I saw three sandhill cranes and many Pacific loons on the river today. Ravens and gulls were also numerous. The water is alive with salmon. I reached Noatak Village when the sunlight was golden and long shadows were on the land. A few subsistence nets were set out near the village but on the whole, things were pretty quiet. Most of the men are gone. They are commercial salmon fishing in Kotzebue Sound. Children played on the dirt road; a three-wheeler ATV scooted by occasionally. A few women and old men are walking in the late evening. Nobody seemed too surprised to see my shaggy form and some even greeted me warmly. I talk to some residents who said the sun was still too warm to dry fish. The worms (fly maggots) would be bad. They fished throughout September and the catch is used to feed the dogs. That is why the chum is also known as the dog salmon. Now the snowmobile has made it easier. They can go to Kotzebue and back in only a day. With dogs it takes two. They work with dogs less now so less fish is needed. Each family used to have at least nine dogs.

I took some pictures but was disappointed to find the store closed. No candy bars for me. It was getting late and I needed to find a campsite before dark so I get back on the river. Paddling in the calm

evening and afterglow of the sunset is pleasing. It is cool. A few miles below the village, I stop to camp on a high bar. The stars shown tonight—Cassiopeia, the Dippers, others—and it is the first time I have seen them on this trip because of the near constant daylight of the arctic summer. I traveled 60 miles today.

August 17, seven weeks out, and it is my birthday. I am 38 years old. Where did all that time go? Clear skies and the cool wind bites at my fingers. The hazy morning turns into a hot afternoon. I am down to a T-shirt by the time I stopped for lunch. I saw a loon that may have been a yellow-billed but it was difficult to be sure. Its bill was light-colored, distinguishing it from a common loon. I meet an Inupiat family in two motorboats. They ask me if I have seen any salmon and I assure them there are plenty. The wind is continuous until the afternoon when it becomes still. The braided river is swift at first but loses most of its velocity when it coalesces into one channel. I stop and investigate Nauyoaruk, an abandon settlement on the river. The wood buildings are solid. There appears to be living quarters and something that looks like a stable. A stable in this country? I was baffled and never found out the

history of the place. Several miles beyond this, I stop at the Sikusuilaq Springs Fish Hatchery. It is located here because of its namesake springs that provides the hatchery with a constant source of pure, fresh water.

The hatchery uses 4,000 gallons per minute (8.9 cfs). Run by the Alaska Department of Fish and Game (ADF&G), it is experimental at this stage, only rearing about four million chum salmon. They are expecting their first return of hatchery-reared salmon this year. When in full production, 40 million fish will be reared and released. This is strictly to supplement the commercial catch in Kotzebue Sound.

I begin trudging up the long, steep walkway from the river and what seems like hundreds of dogs begin to bark. I meet ADF&G biologist Kate Persons who lives at the hatchery with one maintenance worker. They extend a friendly greeting and we talk on the steps of the office building in the warm sun. Kate knows a college friend of mine Debbie Burwin who also works for ADF&G. Kate has her dogs here—about 20 of them. She is an avid dog musher and ran her dogs to Point Barrow last winter. She says she would like to run the Iditarod dogsled race someday.[12] The dogs are fed the salmon carcasses during the egg and sperm take, but not before the fish are cooked, or else there is a danger of the dogs getting roundworms and tapeworms. Kate says she is losing interest in the job because of the isolation and the short time off, which does not allow her to get much farther than Kotzebue. She went on a Hawaiian vacation last October but she wants to be able to get away from the hatchery more often.

The two invited me in for a wonderful birthday dinner of chicken cacciatore with rice—a real home-cooked meal. They also served a good cup of coffee with this. What a shot of caffeine! We talked until the sun was close to the horizon. *Prairie Home Companion* was playing on the radio. I have to find a campsite so I need to depart. Reluctantly I say my goodbyes and head back to the river. The dogs bark. I continue another six miles to the mouth of the Agashashok

---

[12] Kate ran the Iditarod in 1991, 1992, 1993, and 1994. She was awarded Rookie of the Year and placed 11th in 1991, earning her $9,500.

River and want to camp here but too much gravel had built up from the low water and I cannot find a good site. A porcupine waddles by. A mile downstream is a suitable site and I got the tent up just as the sun disappeared under the horizon. It was a damp and chilly evening. Because I paddled late into the evening, I used up a lot of my last intake of carbohydrates. I slept cold this night and my feet would not warm up.

It was cold and foggy the next morning. The 15-mph wind from the northeast added to the chill factor. Everything is damp. I have difficulty trying to start a fire, but succeed and finish off the last of the pancake batter for breakfast. Oatmeal and hot chocolate also help take off the chill. It is possible that I might make Kotzebue today if everything clicks. I hear varied thrushes in the spruce trees behind me. The young are testing their voices. The river rose a few more inches overnight.

Paddling is slow in this still water but the wind is at my back. The fog gradually lifts, revealing the Igichuk Hills on both sides of the river. The roundish hills rise up to craggy peaks and patches of spruce are scattered throughout. The green-and-yellow tundra glows with color in the morning sun. I paddle into the Lower Noatak Canyon. Here the channel narrows and steep banks rise up but the water is deep and clear. And there is no perceptible current. Beyond the canyon, the hills slope to the river and isolated peaks emerge from the tundra.

Subsistence activity increased dramatically below the canyon. I met a member of a large family in a huge red boat who was looking for spotted seals that swim up the river and steal fish from their nets. The family lives on an island near Sakisalnak Point year-round. The river makes a great sweeping bend here and turns south for its last run to the Noatak Delta. What a menagerie of temporary buildings, equipment, boats, and people. All the physical objects and buildings are painted red. I can see most of this entourage on shore as I pass. The man told me that Kotzebue is still 22 miles

from here. The river mouth is 12 miles, indicating that the open water section across Kotzebue Sound is ten miles.

I paddled hard for the rest of the afternoon. The wide, currentless river distorted my perception of distance. Many motorboats are passing me now, most heading toward Kotzebue, perhaps because this is the end of the weekend. It is a gorgeous blue-sky day with the Noatak Delta land flooded in sunlight and delicate, wispy cirrus clouds overhead. As I get closer to the Noatak River mouth, a headwind coming off the ocean becomes stronger. Whitecaps and two-to-three foot waves build up. By the time I reach the mouth, the wind has died, but I am exhausted and do not entertain thoughts of trying to cross the sound at night. I camp in a low, damp area covered with mat willow and Grass-of-Parnassus. I am on Kinuk Island. The sun sets as I prepare dinner. The mosquitoes are thick here but drop off with the disappearing sun. Salmon are jumping all around, producing loud splashes. Birds seem to be more numerous in the delta. I see whimbrels, bar-tailed godwits, and sandhill cranes this evening.

The last challenge of this trip lies before me—the ten-mile open ocean crossing of Hotham Inlet. I can only wonder what tomorrow's weather will bring and if it will allow me to complete my journey.

CHAPTER 9

Open Ocean and the Finish

I wake up before the sunrise. It is August 19. Something inside of me says "Go Now." The sky emanates bloodred in the east. The temperature is well below freezing. Ice had collected on my packs overnight. I break

camp quickly with no breakfast and am on the water in the morning twilight. The coastal hills fall behind me, losing shape as I move to the end of the Noatak Delta. Alarmed tundra swans, sandhill cranes, and ducks break the silence. I move out into open water.

It is calm. Kotzebue floats above the horizon—a mirage caused by distance and light traveling through air layers of different density. Several spotted seals appear while crossing the Sound. They pop their heads out of water,

look around, and slip silently underneath the surface. I paddle past a salmon fishing boat. There are many near the mouth. Everyone aboard is fast asleep. Gulls cry on the wing in the still air.

As the sun rises higher in the sky, the wind freshens. The water becomes choppy, but not threatening. An hour and a half of hard paddling go by and I have moved by a point that I thought would give me protection from the northeast wind. The seas become confused, however, and instead of swells coming from one direction, the waves clash with each other because of crosswinds. There are some tense moments in the next half hour. Am I going to swamp and die a few miles from shore? With great effort, I keep the canoe steady. Time drags. For several seemingly  endless minutes, I do battle with the unpredictable waves but finally the canoe bow rides up on the glorious shoreline. Tension immediately eases. I am safe. Three-foot waves were now hitting the beach as the wind steadily increases.

I leap out of the canoe and drag it ashore, then let out a yell that all of Kotzebue probably heard. I have finished the trip, traversing six hundred and fifty wilderness miles in 51 days. I pace in ecstasy, thanking God, looking around at the splendid green tundra, the big sky, and the blue ocean covered with whitecaps. The wind was in my face and the sun at my back. I am happy. I have had a great adventure and can now be with friends again and tell my story.

The spit of land I was standing on separated the sea from the Kotzebue small boat harbor. I pull the canoe across and paddle safely and leisurely to the boat ramp. I secure my gear and head to the Nu-Luk-Vik Hotel for a biscuits and gravy breakfast and a good cup of coffee. My old supervisor Gill Hall is there with the Northwest Area

(NPS) helicopter pilot and he invites me to the office to talk about my trip.

I wandered around Kotzebue most of the day, including a visit to the National Park office. A friend had sent a check here for me so that I would have money to fly back to Fairbanks. I had called the NPS office to let them know it was coming and asked them to hold it for me, but a misunderstanding had occurred and the check was sent back to my last address. I was penniless. I inquired at the fish processing plant in town for employment, but they did not get enough fish to put on a night shift. This was disappointing, yet I needed a good night's sleep. In the evening, I headed down Lake Street along the waterfront. It was the same as I remembered it. There were lots of tourists and drunk people. I continued to the beach where the fishermen stay during the commercial salmon season. There was a long string of white wall tents up and down the shore. I find an open spot and set up camp. Dinner consists of almonds, chocolate pudding, and canned turkey. Sleep comes quickly. It has been a long and exciting day.

The next morning, I go to the NPS office that administers Noatak National Preserve, Kobuk Valley National Park, and Cape Krusenstern National Monument. I had a long talk with my old supervisor Gill Hall. We cordially aired some past conflicts between us. After this, I described my trip—conditions of travel, the country, and the people I had met. He expressed interest in some of the comments made by visitors and guides. I felt a weight lifted from my shoulders after the meeting. I talked with the NPS resource manager Kate Roney and asked if there were any projects in the field for which I could volunteer but she said there were none. The only opportunity was identifying plants that biologists had collected in the field. Kate was happy to let me do this. Lee Anne was in town and lent me 20 dollars. At last, I could buy some fresh food, although that amount does not go far in Kotzebue. A 25-mph wind from the northeast blew all day and rain started to fall in the evening. I read inside my tent until my back was sore. I got plenty of rest.

No work was available in Kotzebue. For the next six days, I spent my time identifying plants, reading *Moby Dick*, watching videos and movies at the Park Service visitor center, wandering around Kotzebue, and taking walks along the beach. The plants I was examining were collected during the summer by Biological Technician Jim Minnerath.[13] Funding to hire Jim came from the FirePro program. This program is set up to analyze wildland fire history and future potential fire on the landscape using terrain, climate, vegetation that is mapped using satellite images and aerial photography, and plants collected in the field. FirePro analysis is used to determine

appropriate staffing, program support, and funding for each park area where wildland fire may occur. I had seen Jim's name before. It was in the logbook at Abraham Howarth's Nimiuktuk River cabin.

My food was getting low and I very much wanted clean clothes and a hot shower. The weather turned nasty. It became windy, cold, and rainy. On August 23, I ran into Erna and Howard Kantner and their son Seth and his girlfriend. These were friends I had met

---

[13] Jim Minnerath became a Fish and Wildlife Service Wildlife Biologist for the Flint Hill National Wildlife Refuge Kansas in 2000.

on the Kobuk River in 1983. They lived in a semisubterranean igloo on the north bank of the Kobuk, near where the Hunt River enters the larger river. The Kantners invited me in for an arctic char dinner. Susan Bucknell, who I also met that year, dropped in. She is an Alaska Department of Fish and Game (ADF&G) employee, working with the Alaska Game Board and subsistence. It was a grand reunion. Having fished here all summer, the Kantners were rushing around packing and preparing to leave. Erna is headed to Cleveland to visit her family. Howard is headed to the Big Island of Hawaii where they have land and the two will eventually join up for the winter. Seth and his girlfriend were very interested in my trip—where I went, what canoe I used, and what I saw. I felt I was among friends during this enjoyable visit.[14]

The National Outdoor Leadership School (NOLS) party I had met at the headwaters of the Alatna River finally arrived in town. I would run into small groups of them at different places and we would compare our trip adventures. I talked to one group of NOLS people while watching the sunset. They were satisfied with their arctic adventure. Meg Kurtagh, who lives in Homer, quit her lab technician job to go on the trip. She will do more exploring this autumn. She chose NOLS because she didn't want to do the trip alone. The group spent their last night at the hotel and left on August 25. That evening, I took pictures of the colorful floats and other fishing equipment lying out on the beach.

Most of the fishermen were in various stages of packing. The fishing season was winding down. I strolled over to see Derek Craighead, another friend I met in 1983.[15] He was working on a

---

[14] Seth Kantner has since become an established writer and photographer, having written the critically acclaimed book *Ordinary Wolves* in 2004, a novel loosely based on his life along the Kobuk River.

[15] Derek Craighead is Founder and President of Craighead Berengia South based in Kelly, Wyoming.

caribou project, tracking radio-collared animals using satellites. They were presently in the process of ground truthing computer-generated vegetation maps based on Landsat satellite images to delineate caribou habitat. It was a family affair. I met Johnny Craighead, Derek's brother, at the tent entrance. Later he introduced me to his father, Dr. John Craighead, who had emerged from the tent. Dr. Craighead was famous for the research he did with his twin brother, Frank, on Yellowstone National Park's grizzly bears between 1959-1971. Derek came out later and we exchanged warm greetings, not having seen each other for several years. The small get together starts to grow. Lee Anne arrives along with some other park employees as did a Fish and

Wildlife Service employee. Subsistence people who lived on the Kobuk River wandered over. Dr. John offered me a beer. Caribou steaks were put on the grill. I ate well this night. It was somewhat of a farewell gathering. Johnny was leaving in the morning, Dr. Craighead in a few days later, and Derek in a week. Good food was served and quiet conversation murmured over the cracks and pops of the little fire. As the sun nears the horizon, long shadows crept across the land. The sunset intensifies. I talk with Dr. John about bear encounters we have had in Katmai National Park.[16] He relates how he had been chased up a tree by a Yellowstone grizzly. We discuss the difference between brown and grizzly bears, which are now considered the same species. A memorable Arctic evening.

The next day, I went to the NPS office and identified plants for most of the morning and afternoon. Gary Ahlstrand, Alaska

---

[16] Dr. John Craighead died Sept. 18, 2016, at the age of 100.

Regional Office Scientist, was there. He was friendly and we had a good conversation. We talked about my trip, FirePro computer programming, and projects involving air and water quality that were going to be implemented in Alaska parks. Later on, I portage my canoe to the airport and send it to Fairbanks for only 22 dollars (wrote a check). Mark Air had this unbelievably low price because there is very little cargo available to be sent back to the major population centers. I was catching the backhaul to move my canoe. The following day, a letter came for me general delivery at the Kotzebue Post Office. It was a birthday card from my mother and a generous check that would be enough to get me to Fairbanks. My reaction was immediate. I rushed to my tent and packed, despite the driving rain, and headed to the NPS office. I left Lee Anne the 20 dollars I owed her. Sam Eischeid was there. Sam had been brought out of the field because of a disagreement with her supervisor. She was upset and we talked a long time. Then she helped me get my things together and over to the airport. I purchased my ticket to Fairbanks and wanted to return to the office to say goodbyes, but the plane was boarding and I could not take the chance of missing it. I hugged Sam and walked to the plane.

Mount McKinley (now Denali) was out in all its glory as we flew past it on the way to Anchorage. Great glaciers snaked down the rugged southern slopes and through the vast timbered wilderness below. I had to fly to Anchorage because there were no direct flights from Kotzebue to Fairbanks. The hop to Fairbanks was quick, and I was heading to a friend's place on Mad Cap Lane by 1:00 p.m. where my truck was stored. He was not home but the truck started with some coaxing.

I picked up my mail and went to the university to take a shower and do my laundry. That evening, I went to the Blue Marlin pizza restaurant. Miraculously, I bump into two friends Brandon and Nancy Anderson. We talk about my trip in detail. They were quite interested in how it went. They had been leading educational trips in the Alaska wilderness and had several trip possibilities for next summer. Brandon was also trying to get into the Alaska State Trooper Law Enforcement Academy.[17] It was good to be back among friends. The journey was complete. I was home again.[18]

---

[17] Brandon Anderson graduated from the Alaska State Trooper Academy August 31, 1990. After 21 years in Alaska Law Enforcement, he retired from the State Troopers on May 31, 2007.

[18] I left Alaska in late September to work in Everglades National Park, but returned in the spring of 1986 to be a law enforcement ranger in Denali National Park and Preserve.

APPENDIX 1

Wildlife Observations of the Expedition

MAMMALS

Rodentia

Arctic Ground Squirrel *Spermophilus undulatus*

Red Squirrel *Tamiasciurus hudsonicus*

Beaver *Castor canadensis*

Carnivora

Gray Wolf *Canis lupus*

Red Fox *Vulpes vulpes* (including Cross Fox)

Grizzly Bear *Ursus arctos*

Black Bear *Ursus americanus*

Mustelidae

Wolverine *Gulo gulo*

Artiodactyla

Moose *Alces alces*

Caribou *Rangifer tarandus*

Phocidae
Spotted Seal *Phoca largha* In the lower Noatak and Kotzebue Sound

AMPHIBIANS
Wood Frog *Rana sylvatica*

FISH
Northern Dolly Varden *Salvelinus malma malma*
Arctic Grayling *Thymallus arcticus*
Lake Trout *Salvelinus namaycush*
Round Whitefish *Prosopium cylindraceum*
Burbot *Lota lota*
Chum Salmon *Oncorhynchus keta*
Northern Pike *Esox lucius*
Longnose Sucker *Catostomus catostomus*

INSECTS
Ants *Hymenoptera*
Black Flies *Diptera - Simuliidae*
Bees *Hymenoptera*
Beetles *Coleoptera*
Caddisflies *Trichoptera*
Crane Flies *Diptera - Tipulidae*
Horse Flies *Diptera - Tadanidae*
Mayflies *Ephemeroptera*
Midges *Diptera - Chironomidae*
Mosquitoes *Diptera - Culicidae*
Stone Flies *Plecoptera*

BIRDS

Gaviiformes

Red-Throated Loon *Gavia stellata*
Pacific Loon *Gavia pacifica*
Common Loon *Gavia immer*
Yellow-Billed Loon *Gavia adamsii*

Anseriformes

Tundra Swam *Cygnus columbianus*
Canada Goose *Branta canadensis*
Mallard *Anas platyrhynchos*
Northern Pintail *Anas acuta*
American Wigeon *Mareca americana*
Northern Shoveler *Spatula clypeata*
Green-Winged Teal *Anas carolinensis*
Greater Scaup *Aythya marila*
Bufflehead *Bucephala albeola*
Common Eider *Somateria mollissima*
Long-Tailed Duck *Clangula hyemalis*
Harlequin Duck *Histrionicus histrionicus*
Common Goldeneye *Bucephala clangula*
Surf Scoter *Melanitta perspicillata*
Red-Breasted Merganser *Mergus serrator*
Common Merganser *Mergus merganser*

Accipitriformes

Bald Eagle *Haliaeetus leucocephalus*
Osprey *Pandion haliaetus*
Rough-Legged Hawk *Buteo lagopus*
Northern Harrier *Circus hudsonius*

Falconiformes
Merlin *Falco columbarius*
Peregrine Falcon *Falco peregrinus*

Galliformes
Willow Ptarmigan *Lagopus lagopus*
Spruce Grouse *Canachites canadensis*

Gruiformes
Sandhill Crane *Grus canadensis*

Charadriiformes
Semipalmated Plover *Charadrius semipalmatus*
American Golden Plover *Pluvialis dominica*
Wilson's Snipe *Gallinago delicata*
Whimbrel *Numenius phaeopus*
Lesser Yellowlegs *Tringa flavipes*
Spotted Sandpiper *Actitis macularia*
Ruddy Turnstone *Arenaria interpres*
Whimbrel *Numenius phaeopus*
Red-Necked Phalarope *Phalaropus lobatus*
Parasitic Jaeger *Stercorarius parasiticus*
Long-Tailed Jaeger *Stercorarius longicaudus*
Glaucous Gull *Larus hyperboreus*
Herring Gull *Larus argentatus*
Mew Gull *Larus canus*
Herring Gull *Larus argentatus*
Bonaparte's Gull *Chroicocephalus philadelphia*
Arctic Tern *Sterna paradisaea*
Bar-Tailed Godwit *Limosa lapponica*
Upland Sandpiper *Bartramia longicauda* Upper Alatna River Valley

Srigiformes
Short-Eared Owl *Asio flammeus*
Hawk Owl *Bartramia longicauda*
Great Horned Owl *Bubo virginianus*

Piciformes
Northern Flicker *Colaptes auratus*

Alcediniformes
Belted Kingfisher *Ceryle alcyon*

Passeriformes
Alder Flycatcher *Empidonax alnorum*
American Pipit *Anthus rubescens*
American Robin *Turdus migratorius*
Swainson's Thrush *Catharus minimus*
Hermit Thrush *Catharus guttatus*
Varied Thrush *Ixoreus naevius*
Gray Jay *Perisoreus canadensis*
Common Redpoll *Carduelis flammea*
Savannah Sparrow *Ammodramus sandwichensis*
Tree Sparrow *Spizelloides arborea*
White-Crowned Sparrow *Zonotrichia leucophrys*
Dark-Eyed Junco *Junco hyemalis*
White-Crowned Sparrow *Zonotrichia leucophrys*
Northern Wheatear *Oenanthe oenanthe*
Northern Shrike *Lanius borealis*
Common Raven *Corvus corax*
Bohemian Waxwing *Bombycilla garrulus*
Arctic Warbler *Phylloscopus borealis*
Yellow-Rumped Warbler *Setophaga coronata*

Cliff Swallow *Petrochelidon pyrrhonota*
Tree Swallow *Tachycineta bicolor*
Bank Swallow *Riparia riparia*
Black-Capped Chickadee *Poecile atricapillus*
Boreal Chickadee *Poecile hudsonicus*
Rusty Blackbird *Euphagus carolinus*

Podicipediformes
Red-Necked Grebe *Podiceps grisegena*

APPENDIX 2

Flora Observed on the Expedition

FAMILY/SPECIES
Sphagnidae
Sphagnum Moss *Sphagnum sp.*
Ascomycetidae
Lichens

Equisetaceae
Equisetum sp.

Lycopodiaceae
Lycopodium sp.

Polypodiaceae
Ferns

Pinaceae
Tamarack *Larix laricina* (Du Roi) K. Koch
White Spruce *Picea glauca* Moench Voss
Black Spruce *Picea mariana* P. Mill. BSP.

Gramineae
Grasses

Cyperaceae
Sedges *Carex sp.*
Cottongrass *Eriophorum sp.*

Liliaceae
Wild Chive *Allium schoenoprasum* L.
Alpine lily *Lloydia serotina* L. Rchb.

Melanthiaceae
Mountain Deathcamas *Anticlea elegans* Pursh Rydb.

Salicaceae
Balsam Poplar *Populus balsamifera* L.
Quaking Aspen *P. tremuloides* Michx.
Reticulated Willow *Salix reticulata* L.
Feltleaf Willow *S. alaxensis* Anderss. Cov.
Other Willows *Salix sp.*

Polygonaceae
Bistort *Polygonum bistorta* L.

Betulaceae
Dwarf Birch *B. glandulosa* Michx.
Green Alder *Alnus crispa* Ait. Pursh

Ranunculaceae
Marsh-Marigold *Caltha palustris* L.
Monkshood *Aconitum delphinifolium* DC.

Papaveraceae
Arctic Poppy *Papaver lapponicum* Tolm. Nordh.

Saxifragaceae
Grass-of-Parnassus *Parnassia palustris* L.
Prickly Saxifrage *Saxifraga tricuspidata* Rottb.
Saxifrage *Saxifrage sp.* L.
Alaska Boykinia *Boykinia richardsonii* Hook. Gray

Rosaceae
White Mountain-Avens *Dryas integrifolia* M. Vahl
Yellow Mountain Avens *Dryas drummondii* Richards
Marsh Fivefinger *Potentilla palustris* L. Scop.
Cloudberry *Rubus chamaemorus* L.
Nagoonberry *R. arcticus* L.
Alaska Spiraea *Spiraea Beauverdiana* Schneid.
Rose *Rosa acicularis* Lindl.

Leguminosae
Alpine Milk-Vetch *Astragalus alpinus* L.
Wild Sweet-Pea *Hedysarum mackenzii* Richards.
Oxytropis *Oxytropis nigrescens* Pall. Fisch.

Pyrolaceae
Pyrola *Pyrola asarifolia* Michx.

Empetraceae
Crowberry *Empetrum nigrum* L.

Onagraceae
Fireweed *Epilobium angustifolium* L.
Dwarf Fireweed *E. latifolium* L.

Cornaceae
Bunchberry *Cornus canadensis* L.

Pyrolaceae
Pyrola *Pyrola grandiflora* Radius

Ericaceae
Bog-Rosemary *Andromeda polifolia* L.
Alpine Bearberry *Arctostaphylos alpina* L. Spreng.
Kinnikinick *A. uva-ursi* L. Spreng.
Dwarf Labrador Tea *Ledum palustre decumbens* L. Hult.
Labrador Tea *Ledum palustre groenlandicum* L. Oeder Hult.
Alpine Azalea *Loiseleuria procumbens* L. Desv.
Bog Blueberry *Vaccinium uliginosum occidentale* (A.Gray) Hult.
Lowbush Cranberry *V. vitis-idaea* L
Bog Cranberry *Oxycoccus microcarpus* Turez

Menyanthaceae
Bog-Bean *Menyanthes trifoliata* L.

Orobanchaceae
Purple Paintbrush *Castilleja caudata Pennell* Rebr.
Labrador Lousewort *Pedicularis labradorica* Wirsing
Woolly Lousewort *Pedicularis lanata* Cham. Schltdl.
Sudeten Lousewort *Pedicularis sudetica* Willd.

Lentibulariaceae
Butterwort *Pinguicula vulgaris* L.

Caprifoliaceae
Twinflower *Linnaea borealis* L.
High Bush Cranberry *Viburnum edule* Michx. Raf.

Polemoniaceae

Jacob's Ladder *Polemonium acutiflorum* Willd.

Asteraceae

Aster *Aster sibiricus* L.

Pussy's Toe *Antannaria friesiana* Trautv. Ekman

Alpine Arnica *Arnica alpina* L. Olin

Fleabane *Erigeron sp.*

Sweet Coltsfoot *Petasites sagittatus* Banks Gray

Saussurea *Saussurea angustifolia* Willd. DC.

Lacerate Dandelion *Taraxacum lacerum* Greene

Arnica *Arnica frigida* C. A. May.

References

The Alaska Geographic Society. 1981. The Kotzebue Basin. Alaska Geographic. Vol. 8 No. 3. 183 p.

Armstrong, R.H. 1995. Guide to the Birds of Alaska (4th ed.). Alaska Northwest Books. Anchorage, AK. 323 p.

Behnke, R. J. 2002. Trout and Salmon of North America. The Free Press. New York, NY. 359 p.

Connor, C. 2014. Roadside Geology of Alaska (2nd ed.). Mountain Press Publishing Company. Missoula, MT. 317 p.

DeCicco, A.L. 1985. Inventory and Cataloging of Sport Fish and Sport Fish Waters of Western Alaska with Emphasis on Arctic Char Life History. Alaska Department of Fish and Game.

Federal Aid in Fish Restoration Annual Performance Report 1984-1985, Project F-9-17, Volume 26: 41-134.

DeCicco, A.L. 1992. Long Distance Movements of Anadromous Dolly Varden between Alaska and the U.S.S.R. Arctic 45:120-123.

Ehrlich, P.R., D.S. Dobkin, and D. Wheye. 1988. The Birder's Handbook: A Field Guide to the Natural History of North American Birds. Simon & Schuster/Fireside Books. New York, NY. 785 p.

Grybeck, D., M.P. Brosge, I.L. Tailleur, and C.G. Mull. 1977. Geologic Map of the Brooks Range, Alaska. U.S. Geological Survey Open-File Report 77-1668, scale 1,000,000.

Hulten, E. 1968. Flora of Alaska and Neighboring Territories. University of Stanford. Stanford, CA. 1008 p.

References

Kessel, B. 1989. Birds of the Seward Peninsula, Alaska. University of Alaska Press. Fairbanks, AK. 330 p.

Kunz, M. 2005 The Denbigh Flint Complex at Punyik Point, Etivlik Lake, Alaska. *Alaska Journal of Anthropology* 3(2):101–116

Morrow, J.E. 1980. The Freshwater Fishes of Alaska. Alaska Northwest Publishing Co. Anchorage, AK. 248 p.

Nelson, R.K., K.H. Mautner, and G.R. Bane. 1982. Tracks in the Wildland: A Portrayal of Koyukon and Nunamiut Subsistence. University of Alaska Fairbanks. Fairbanks, AK. 465 p.

Nelson, S.W. and D. Grybeck. 1980. Geologic Map of the Survey Pass Quadrangle, Brooks Range, Alaska 1/250,000. Miscellaneous Field Studies. MAP MF—1176-A. US Geological Survey. Washington D. C.

Orth, D.J. 1967. Dictionary of Alaska Place Names. USGS Professional Paper 567. U.S. Geological Survey, U.S. Printing Office, Washington D.C. 1083 p.

Wild Edible and Poisonous Plants of Alaska. 1989. Cooperative Extension Unit, University of Alaska Fairbanks. Fairbanks, AK. 91 p.

Williss, G.L 1985. "Do Things Right the First Time": Administrative History. The National Park Service and the Alaska National Interest Lands Conservation Act of 1980. U.S. National Park Service. GPO. Washington D.C. 322 p.

Young, S.B. 1989. To the Arctic: An Introduction to the Far Northern World. John Wiley & Sons Inc. New York, NY. 354 p.